# The Fabric Guide
# for People Who Sew

# The Fabric Guide for People Who Sew

by Fenya Crown

**GROSSET & DUNLAP**
A National General Company
Publishers         New York

Library of Congress Catalog Number: 72-90860

ISBN: 0-448-01310-X (Trade Edition)
ISBN: 0-448-13164-1 (Library Edition)
First Printing
Printed in the United States of America

# Contents

*Illustrations follow page* **106**

# The Fabric Guide
# for People Who Sew

**I**

# *My Romance with Fabrics*

SOME PEOPLE CAN spend hours browsing in a book store. Others can lose themselves inspecting wine collections in a well-stocked liquor store. I'm a fabric-lover.

My romance with textiles began as a teen-ager in the early 1930s when I started making my own clothes and haunted the local remnant stores. It blossomed when I became a professional dress designer in the late 1940s and graduated to the luxury of handling all the newest fabrics in the textile manufacturers' display rooms. The passion was rekindled when, in researching material for this book, I found some strikingly beautiful and useful new fabrics that are coming onto the scene for the 1970s.

Like most romances, this one has had some disappointments. Sometimes my expectations about a fabric were too high. Sometimes it didn't live up to its promises. Sometimes my ignorance about a fabric and how to handle it were to blame.

3

One purpose of this book is to help others who sew avoid these pitfalls. It will provide an understanding of how the various apparel textiles behave and why, and some guidelines to shopping, sewing and cleaning them. Some technical explanations are essential but I have kept these to a minimum.

I am grateful for the cooperation of many individuals, companies and textile industry associations which supplied information for this book. For information about the natural fibers I wish to thank the Wool Bureau, the International Silk Association, the Japan Silk Association, the China National Textiles Import and Export Corporation, the National Cotton Council, the Irish Linen Guild and the Belgian Linen Association; for synthetic fibers and fabrics, Celanese Corporation, E. I. du Pont de Nemours and Company, Eastman Chemical Products, Monsanto Textiles Company, American Enka Company, Hoechst Fibers, Incorporated, Beaunit Textiles and Burlington Industries; for special fibers and fabrics, the Armo Company, Pellon Corporation, Owens-Corning Fiberglas Corporation and Borg Textiles. A special thank-you to the Federal Trade Commission for information in the chapter on labeling regulations, and another to my husband, who patiently double-checked the facts and figures.

# II
# The Fabric-Fashion Revolution

A FASHION REVOLUTION is in progress in the United States, its main impetus a reawakened interest in home sewing. More than forty million American women are now estimated to be involved with this form of creative self-expression. At least half of them are teen-agers and women in their early twenties.

Simultaneously we are witnessing a revolution in fabrics which demands of the woman who makes her own clothes an understanding of textiles—their many varieties, their individual properties, how to handle them in sewing and design, how to recognize quality in a fabric, how to care for each type.

The grandmothers of this generation of home sewers only had to know about cotton, wool, silk, linen and rayon, and they learned easily from experience. But more than half of the women who sew today—those under thirty—have lived their entire lives in the "synthetic age" that began in 1939 with the commercial introduction of nylon.

Today the fabrics created from man-made fibers are dominant. The combinations of fibers, textures and finishes are literally uncountable. Synthetics are blended with one another and with the natural fibers (cotton, wool, silk, linen) to combine the advantages of each. New or improved fabrics are constantly coming on the market. New processes and finishes—which give fabrics special textures, preshrink them, make them water-repellent, stretchable, permanently pleated or pressed—have further multiplied the choices.

And so this book—to provide some basic guidelines to serve in place of the uncertainties of trial-and-error fabric buying.

## How the Revolution Came About

Some of the causes of the fashion/fabric revolution were social, paralleling changes in life style. Some were economic, some technological. The beginnings go back to the end of World War II.

When that war ended in 1945, worldwide textile production had dropped sharply due to wartime dislocations and the exhaustion of such large textile-producing countries as Germany and Japan. In the United States, where the decline was less severe, there was an enormous pent-up demand for clothing fabrics. Because of military needs, these had been strictly rationed to manufacturers of civilian clothes, with regulations that limited, for example, the length and width of skirts. The federal controls were designed to limit the amount of fabric manufacturers could use for civilian clothes, since the military required vast amounts of cloth. There was no individual rationing of fabric or clothes, as there was for many types of food. A large percentage of women were making their own clothes, as they always had.

A sort of fashion boredom had set in and American women were more than ready for style changes when the freeze was lifted. Then, in 1947, came Christian Dior's radical new look of long, twirling skirts. The effect was to start an expansion of the women's clothing industry so great that by the 1950s home sewing seemed to be becoming an obsolete art. A whole generation grew up knowing nothing of the skills and satisfactions of creating their own wardrobes.

A contributing factor to the new popularity of manufactured dresses was that cotton—previously pretty much restricted to house dresses and aprons—began to be styled for street wear, and the manufactured fashions were available at very low cost. For example, one dress I designed in 1950 retailed at $5.95 and could be seen on the main street of any major city in the United States. To illustrate how popular daytime cotton dresses became, this one used about three-quarters of a million yards of fabric during its life span.

In the meantime, the new synthetics became commercially available, to a large extent eliminating the necessity for time-consuming hand washing and elaborate ironing. For a while it looked as though we were heading for an age of pushbutton-manufactured apparel.

It was in the mid-1960s that the home sewing revolution began. It started with the young—teen-agers rebelling against dictated styles and determined enough about expressing their individual ideas through their clothes to learn how to sew. Their social environment encouraged this individualism. The rapid increases in prices of ready-made clothes caused young adults also to turn to the sewing machine and older women to use their former skills. Thus the home-sewing industry was born.

## Buying Power Counts

The enormous buying power of the new millions of women who make their own clothes has brought about big changes in the availability of fabrics. For a quarter-century after World War II, the apparel textile industry concentrated on supplying manufacturers of ready-made clothes, for the simple economic reason that a manufacturer may use thousands of yards of a single pattern while a home sewer will buy only a few yards at a time. As a result, most retail fabric stores were largely dependent on "mill ends," or remnants from these manufacturers, or on imports from other countries where home dressmaking has always been a way of life.

Today, however, most of the major textile companies have special over-the-counter departments devoted to designing and producing fabrics for retail sale. For the most part, the old remnant stores are being replaced by modern departments or fabric shops stocking a wide variety of quality goods. In 1967, there were a little more than two thousand fabric stores across the United States; in 1973, there were approximately twelve thousand.

Prices of fabrics can vary a great deal, even if they are of the same fiber and weave or knit. A domestic woven cotton, such as gingham, may sell for less than

$2 a yard; an imported Swiss or Italian sateen (printed) may be between $8 and $10 a yard. Prices of synthetics fluctuate just as widely. A polyester-cotton blend may be priced between $1 and $2 a yard, while a double-knit jacquard or striped polyester may be close to $10, especially if imported from Belgium or Germany. Silks and wools also vary greatly, anywhere from $4 a yard to astronomical figures for heavy silks and rare wools.

Variety of choice is important since the fabric is the essential factor in the design and appearance of the clothes you make. You can use your *individual* buying power in this connection. For those who can't find the type of fabric they want in their local shops, this book includes a list of major wholesale resources that supply fabrics to retail stores at the end of each chapter dealing with a specific type of fabric. Your store should be able to get the desired material for you from these sources, since the manufacturers are now very conscious of the home-sewing market. I should stress that these wholesalers will not sell directly to individuals, but only to the store.

Fabric stores carry merchandise because it is profitable, rather than to provide convenience and variety for the consumer. But they can be educated if you, the customer, are determined to get what you want. You can write to the resources mentioned in this book to get a list of retail stores in your area that carry the fabric you want. Or, you can take the list to your local fabric store and ask to speak to the buyer. Or, you can simply request that the person in charge make an effort to obtain the fabric you want. Improvements won't happen overnight, but by-the-yard departments can be upgraded by consumer or competitive pressure.

# When You're Shopping for Fabrics

The properties of the various types of fabrics are covered in the individual chapters, and the federal labeling regulations are summarized in Chapter IV, but here are a few general commonsense suggestions on shopping for yard goods.

• If you are a new home sewer shopping for your first fabric, judging the quality of a fabric by its "hand" (how it feels when you touch it) may be puzzling. Each type of fabric has its own special properties. Wool should be soft and resilient when crushed in the hand. Some cottons are crisp, some are silky, depending on type. The feel should tell you if this fabric is what you are after. The same applies to crushproof synthetic fabrics. There should be no creases after you release a fistful of cloth. The better the fabrics perform, the higher the quality of the cloth.

• If the fabric is to serve the purpose for which you are buying it, you have to know what it is made of and just how it launders, cleans and irons. U.S. government regulations require labels identifying the content of the fabric, specific instructions on care and, if imported, the country of origin. There are some exceptions applying to remnants or "mill ends," i.e., small pieces not on a bolt.

• A well-known trademark may be a good indication of quality because the synthetic-fiber producers require that certain standards be met in all fabrics carrying their trademarks.

## Some Notes about Imported Fabrics

Clothing fabrics were among the earliest articles of international trade. During the time of the Roman Empire, silks coming from Asia were equated with gold. England built a large part of its mercantile empire on textile exports. Australia's early commercial development was largely based on wool.

In the United States today, imports from all over the world are available in fabric shops. In fact, about half of all fabrics sold for home sewing come from overseas. This variety is a great fashion boon to the home sewer who wants to design something different—although imported fabrics are generally more expensive.

(The fabrics will be labeled with country of origin.)

Each country has something special to offer. Great Britain always has been noted—and still is today—for its classic wools (tartans, plaids, tweeds) and cotton Liberty prints, which currently are much in vogue again. British fabrics generally provide good value for the money.

France's specialties are its luxurious couture-type fabrics, mainly in the natural fibers—silks, cottons and wools. These high-fashion fabrics are in the more expensive price ranges. However, some of the big-name French fabric houses, such as Abraham, which specialize in original prints of great beauty, have been considering putting out moderately priced lines for the American home-sewing market. Also widely available to the American home sewer are quality French printed cottons made by such houses as Boussac.

Italian fabrics are noted primarily for the innovative use of natural fibers—for example, in double knit wools and very fine cotton knits—and for a creative approach to prints and other finishes. Limited production of these specialty Italian fabrics makes them expensive, but they are among the most interesting imports for the woman who wants the unusual for her designs.

Switzerland supplies us with delicate cottons and sheers and embroidered fabrics. From Ireland and Belgium come the pure linens. It may be surprising to many that Germany is probably the most important producer of synthetic fibers in Europe today. German fabrics are of high quality and are competitively priced. German specialties include knitted polyesters in the flatter, lighter weights, jacquard knits and novelty knit cottons, which make up into chic dresses and sportswear with unusual shape retention.

Japanese imports provide a great variety of all fabrics. As far as the sewing public is concerned, the best-known Japanese specialty is brocades. For the rest, Japanese fabrics are competitive in styling and price with American mass-produced products.

With the easing of restrictions on trade with China—the original home of silk—both cultivated and wild silk Chinese fabrics will again be available to the American consumer. This may bring back all the old favorites such as tussah, pongee and other famous Chinese silks.

Foreign specialties aside, the American home sewer will probably find the widest selection of types and styles of fabrics in the U.S.-made textiles, particularly the synthetics, in which the United States leads the world.

The U.S. textile mill consumption of man-made fibers almost tripled between 1960 and 1970 and cotton and wool production fell off sharply. But a trend worth noting is the renewed attention the home-sewing public is paying to the natural fiber textiles. Whether this is related to the environmental movement or due to the changeableness of fashion is difficult to judge. Whatever the reason, the trend is a welcome one. The synthetics have made big changes in our way of living, but the world of fabrics would be much less exciting without the variety of natural cottons, wools, silks and linens that have made our clothes comfortable and luxurious for thousands of years.

# ✸III

# *From Fiber to Fabric*

EVERY PIECE OF cloth has a character of its own. As in human beings, this character is partly inherited, partly a result of what happens as it is developing.

Two fabrics of the same name may be as far removed in personality and appearance as fifth and sixth cousins. And two cloths of completely different origin may be made to resemble each other so closely that only textile experts can tell them apart.

How do fabrics get their individual properties, textures, designs, colors and finishes?

It all starts with the fiber, which can be either a tiny wisp of plant or animal matter (as in cotton and wool) or a long and very fine threadlike filament (as in silk and man-made synthetics). It is the fiber that gives the cloth its "genetic" properties—the softness and absorbency of cotton, the warmth and insulation of wool, the sleekness of silk, the strength of nylon, the wash-

and-wear properties of polyester, the wool-like characteristics of acrylic.

There are four main natural fibers used in apparel textiles: cotton, plucked from the boll of the cotton plant; wool, sheared from the backs of sheep and certain other animals; flax (linen), extracted from the stem of the flax plant; and silk, spun in long filaments by the silkworm.

Nineteen manufactured, or synthetic, fibers have been given generic names in the United States under the Textile Fiber Products Identification Act. Of these nineteen, only seven are basic apparel textile fibers: acetate and triacetate, acrylic and modacrylic, nylon, polyester and rayon. Two—spandex and anidex—are used in stretch fabrics. Six fibers are used largely in nonapparel fabrics: glass, metallic (except in small amounts for glitter and trim), olefin, rubber, saran and vinyon. Four are not currently manufactured in the United States: azlon, lastrile, nytril and vinal.

The man-made synthetics divide into two categories: (1) cellulosic (rayon, acetate and triacetate), which are produced mainly from cellulose, the substance of all plant life; (2) noncellulosic, or totally manufactured from chemical elements taken variously from petroleum and natural gas, coal, air, water, alcohol, limestone.

While all fibers of the same name have properties in common, they may be no more identical than members of a large family. Nylon, for example, may mean an ultrathin fiber that is processed into the sheerest hose, or a heavy thread used to give strength to automobile tires. The acrylic carpet bears no resemblance to your favorite sweater, although they can be made of the same fiber.

## Long and Short Fibers

There are two basic types of fibers: *staple* and *filament*. Each type lends different properties to the finished fabrics.

The name staple applies to all short fibers, which can be any length from one-quarter inch, used for flocking, to eighteen inches, in some rare wools. The most common length is one and a half inches, the average length of cotton fiber. Cotton, wool and flax are always in staple form only.

Man-made fibers, which are manufactured in continuous filament form, can also be cut up into staple lengths. Synthetics that are blended with cotton are cut into one-and-one-half-inch lengths to correspond to the average length of the cotton staple used in these blends.

The filament fibers include silk and virtually all the man-made synthetics. The silkworm extrudes its fine filaments in lengths of about 2,500 feet, through an orifice known as a spinneret. Imitating the silkworm,

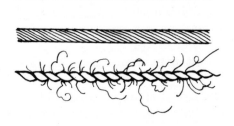

*Forms of man-made fibers*

the man-made filament fibers also are formed by forcing a thick, syrupy mixture through perforations in a spinneret—but here the mixture is a chemical one, the spinneret is a modern piece of machinery, and the fibers are manufactured in a continuous twenty-four–hour flow. Most fiber-producing companies never stop their spinnerets unless there is a power failure or the machines need cleaning.

The filament fibers generally are processed into the dressy fabrics that require smoothness, sheen and good drapeability. The staple fibers produce fabrics that are more porous, and provide coolness when needed or bulk for warmth, softness to the touch and a variety of textures.

As we shall note, though, there are many ways of engineering man-made fibers and yarns, and hundreds of different types of fabrics can be derived from the filament yarns or fibers.

## How a Synthetic Fiber Is Created

To see how these differences come about, let's take a look at the creation of a synthetic fiber and its development into textile. Since the processes are complex and have many variations, we'll stick to the most important steps that are common to all man-made fibers.

The chemical elements that are to form the fiber are combined in a polymerization system where they form long chainlike molecules called polymers. In any given family of fibers, the chemical ingredients may be varied, or modified by additives, to give the fiber special properties such as controlled luster or dullness, extra strength, and antistatic qualities.

The syruplike mixture is now forced through the tiny holes of a spinneret (which resembles a shower head), which may have as few as ten holes or as many as several thousand, depending on the end use of the fiber. The sizes and shapes of the spinneret holes also will vary, to produce a finer or heavier filament or to give the fiber a multifaceted shape that also modifies its properties.

Now the filament must be hardened. This is done in one of three ways, according to the nature of the synthetic.

• The first method is called *wet spinning*. The spinneret extrudes its mixture into a chemical bath which "regenerates" the actual fiber-making substance out of the syrupy compound. For example, in making rayon by the viscose process, the acid in the bath decomposes the viscose in the mixture and solidifies the cellulose into fine rayon filaments.

• The second method is known as *dry spinning*. This involves drying the mixture in warm air as it emerges from the spinneret and is used when the basic fiber material has been dissolved in a solvent for extrusion, as in acetate. The warm air evaporates the solvent, leaving the acetate filament.

• The third method is called *melt spinning*. This is used when the fiber-forming material—say, nylon or polyester—is molten as it comes out of the spinneret and is hardened by cool air.

No sooner has the synthetic fiber been born than it is being adapted to the purpose for which it was created.

Even while it is hardening—or sometimes after it has hardened—the filament is drawn out and stretched to a precisely controlled degree. This stretching process reduces the diameter of the fiber, but more important,

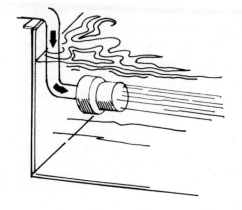

*Wet Spinning*

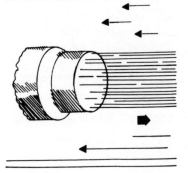

*Dry Spinning*

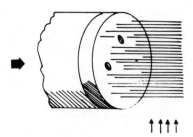

*Melt Spinning*

it changes its strength and resiliency. If the strength of the fiber is increased, the filament's ability to stretch is lessened. The fiber-making company determines the most suitable combination for the yarn and fabric into which the fiber will go.

Synthetic fibers also can be manipulated by chemical or mechanical processes so that they have built-in permanent crimps, or bends, along their length. This is done to give the yarn into which the filaments are twisted a softer, more open and bulky texture, since the crimped filaments will not lie flat against one another in the yarn.

One of the newer ways of doing this is to join two different types of the same synthetic substance along the length of the fiber. When the fiber is processed, it develops a twist because one side shrinks more than the other. This type of fiber, known as *bi-component*, is becoming more and more important commercially because the chemical crimp produces much stronger recovery from stretching than the mechanical process.

## Fiber into Yarn

The fiber is now ready to be made into yarn. To most women the word "yarn" means the wool or synthetic they buy in skeins for home knitting or crocheting. In terms of textiles, it means the basic thread of all fabrics.

There are two principal types of yarn, *filament* and *spun*. Filament yarns are produced by twisting the long filament fibers together. In some cases, a single filament may be the yarn, as in some hose or very sheer woven fabrics. When two or more different filament yarns

—say, silk and polyester—are twisted together, they form what is known as a *combination yarn*. (There are also *combination fabrics* made by weaving or knitting two different types of yarn together.)

Spun yarns are made of short staple fibers. These may be natural fibers—cotton, wool, flax—or synthetic fibers whose filaments are assembled into bundles called "tow" and then are cut up or broken into shorter lengths. The staples are then spun into yarn by spinning machines. Staples of different fibers—natural and synthetic—may be blended together to form what is known as *blended yarn*. The most common blend is polyester and cotton. Because of their shorter fibers, spun yarns are generally more irregular, bulkier and softer than filament yarns.

Because the fiber-producing chemical companies do so much to promote their trade names by advertising, there is a common misconception that they also make fabrics. Not so. Producers like DuPont, Hoechst Fibers, Celanese and other chemical companies that make synthetic fibers usually have other firms do the rest of the work in making textiles. At this writing, however, some chemical companies have announced their intention of going further in the production process, for example, texturizing and spinning the yarns themselves.

But now, most of the chemical companies ship the synthetic fibers out in three forms; (1) as single unbroken filaments wound on giant spools, to be twisted into filament yarns; (2) as ropelike bundles of tow, which is cut into the appropriate staple lengths by the yarn-spinning companies; and (3) as staple, which the chemical company cuts into lengths specified by the customer, the yarn processor.

# Throwing the Yarn

In the processing of modern synthetics, and silk, an important role is played by the *throwing* companies (from the old English word "thraw," to twist). In the section on filament fibers, I said that these generally produced the smooth, dressier fabrics. But by the significant processes known as texturizing or texturing (the job of the "throwsters"), the appearance, and hand of the filament yarns can be changed and they can be given bulk, different surface effects and controlled stretch. Texturizing is used only on filament yarns.

There are at least five methods used today for texturizing synthetics. All involve putting permanent crimps, twists, loops, coils or curls into the otherwise straight and smooth filament yarns. In the man-made fibers, these twists and turns can be locked in by heat, with the result that when the yarn is stretched it tends to remember its new shape and return to it like a coiled spring.

In silk, texturizing is done mainly to make processing of the yarn easier, or to produce a special surface effect, such as the pebbly appearance of crepe. Silk twists are not heat-set. The throwing industry originally got its name from the twisting or throwing of silk.

The importance of texturizing to the consumer lies in the many new types of fabrics it can provide. For example: Texturizing of synthetics was first applied mainly to knit filament yarns. In the late 1950s and through the 1960s, yarns were also texturized for woven fabrics, but these yarns were used primarily in the filling, or width of the fabric (see page 26), while the straight untexturized filament yarns were used in the warp, or lengthwise direction. Today, a wide range of woven synthetic fabrics, from satins to heavy denims, is being produced with texturized yarns running in both directions, giving the previously more rigid wovens some of the comfortable qualities of knits.

Texturizing is a custom process. The throwster will use the method best suited to the type of fabric the textile company plans to manufacture, carefully controlling the amount of bulkiness or stretch and the nature of the surface texture.

## Yarn into Fabric

Besides the throwsters—who are concerned only with the processing of filament yarns—*spinners* and *yarn converters* are also involved in the preparation of yarn for fabrication into cloth. Spinning plants convert the short staple fibers, (either natural or synthetic), into spun yarn on giant spinning machines. Yarn converters, who may also be throwsters, dye or otherwise prepare the yarns for knitting or weaving mills.

Some of the textile companies are fully integrated—that is, they prepare the yarn, make the fabrics, apply the dyes and finishes. Others will sell the fabrics to independent converters in the form of *greige goods* —undyed and unfinished cloth.

The converters are middlemen in the producer-to-consumer flow of textiles. They send the greige goods out to specialized plants for dyeing, printing or finishing and are primarily concerned with design, styling and wholesale distribution of the cloth.

It used to be that each converter concentrated on handling one type of fabric—say, knits, or silk prints, or specialty cottons or suit materials. Today, however, because of the rapid style changes, some of the larger independent converters have diversified and will handle many different types of fabrics.

The converters serve an important fashion purpose in the textile industry. The big mills tend to produce fabrics that can be manufactured and sold in large quantities. The converters, on the other hand, are in position to operate profitably by designing and selling high-fashion fabrics in smaller quantities.

Both the textile-producing companies and the independent converters sell the cloth directly to apparel manufacturers, as well as to retail fabric shops.

## How a Cloth Gets Its Colors and Finishes

The colors that liven up the fabrics you buy may be given to the cloth at any stage of its production. The method used is generally determined by the nature of the fiber, the fabric design to be achieved and the process to be employed in finishing the cloth.

Dyes can be applied to staple fibers before they are spun into yarn (stock-dyed); to the filament fibers while they are still in the chemical solution (solution-dyed); to the synthetic tow before it is cut into staple length (tow-dyed); to the yarn before it is woven or knitted into cloth (yarn-dyed); or to the fabric itself (piece-dyed).

Then there are the prints. The two most common methods of printing colors on fabrics are roller printing and screen printing. The less expensive printed cloths are usually produced by the roller method, which employs a roller engraved with the selected design. It can print thousands of yards of this design in a single run, but is uneconomical if used to print small yardage.

This is where screen printing comes in. It resembles stenciling, and is able to produce more brilliant coloration as well as more difficult designs, such as very large patterns. Today, screen printing is done mostly by machine, but hand printing is by no means obsolete. Hand printing is usually confined, however, to producing designs for the couture, both in Europe and in the United States.

Modern technology is constantly searching out new printing methods. One, the heat-transfer process, involves printing the design on paper, then transferring it to the cloth by special pressing machines under high heat. This process is speedy and very economical. Jet printing, developed in England, employs a form of controlled jet spray on moving cloth to produce an almost infinite variety of designs.

For home sewing, the most important aspects of fabric color and design are that they should please esthetically and be colorfast. There are, however, some end results of different coloring processes that may affect how the cloth should be handled.

For example, regular ginghams, plaids or stripes will usually be woven out of different-colored yarns, which means that either the fiber or the yarn has been dyed. The weaving process produces precise patterns that can easily be matched in sewing. If these same patterns are printed, there may be variations in the design which will make matching difficult. On the other hand, huge oversize plaids or wavy stripes—which require no matching and are hard to produce by weaving—are usually found in dramatic printed fabrics.

Finishes are given to fabrics for many reasons: to firm up or soften the cloth, to change the surface texture, to strengthen some of its weaker characteristics or improve its better ones, to give it special properties.

The finishes may involve either chemical or mechanical processes or both. Typical examples of chemical finishes are durable press and stain resistance; typical mechanical methods include moiréing, flocking and embossing. The widely used finishes also include mercerizing, waterproofing and water repellancy, preshrinking, soil release, wrinkle resistance and flame retardation. The more important special finishes are described in Chapter XV.

## How Fabrics are Made: Wovens and Knits

Virtually all cloth used in apparel today falls into two broad categories: woven and knitted. There are fabrics made by a sort of matting and pressing method, such as felt, but their use in apparel is so limited that they may be ignored here. (See Chapter XVI and Chapter XVII on special fabrics.)

All woven fabrics, no matter how different they may appear, have a fundamentally simple construction. Horizontal yarns (filling) are interlaced at right angles with the vertical yarns (warp) by passing them over and under each other. The fabrics are manufactured on high-speed looms which, among other things, can weave threads of different colors into a wide variety of plaids, checks, stripes, herringbones and other patterns.

There are three basic types of woven fabrics: *plain*, *twill* and *satin*.

• In the *plain weave*, the horizontal threads go over and under alternate vertical threads. Sheeting, denim, chal-

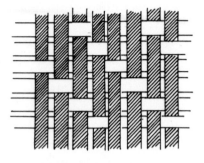

Satin Weave

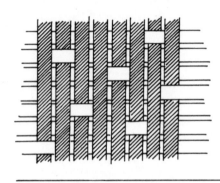

Twill Weave

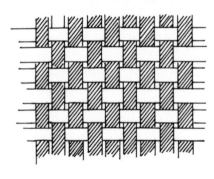

Plain weave

lis, poplin and organdy are some examples of the plain weave.

- The *twill weave* produces the effect of diagonal lines on the surface of the cloth. The lines may be barely discernible, if at all, in such cloths as flat serge or gabardine, or highly visible, as in whipcord. In the twill weave, the filling threads may go over one warp thread and under, say, three others—repeating this sequence for the width of the fabric. Variations of twill are achieved by having the filling threads woven over and under different numbers of warp threads.

- The *satin weave* is actually a variation of the twill, but the diagonal lines are not visible. This is because the horizontal threads go under so many vertical threads at one time that the fabric looks as though it is made of threads running in one direction only. This gives it a smooth, satiny appearance.

Napped and pile fabrics are made by looping an additional filling yarn through the warp and projecting the yarn ends to form the surface. The protruding yarn ends may be cut or left standing, depending on the type of pile desired. Velvets are usually woven face to face and then cut apart; the cut face forms the velvet surface.

Knitted fabrics are constructed by interlocking loops of yarn in a chain, just as your home knitting needles do. But while the home knitter has to make each loop separately, manufactured knits are produced on many different types of versatile machines that can make hundreds of thousands of loops a minute.

Since the construction of the knitted fabric you buy will have a bearing on the garment you make, let's take a look at various forms of knits and how they are made.

Knitted fabrics can be grouped into two broad categories: *weft* (or filling) *knits* and *warp knits*. The primary difference is that in the weft knits the looped chains of yarn run horizontally across the width of the fabric and in the warp knits they run lengthwise.

Weft knits, due to their construction, have a horizontal stretch. The best known of these are unquestionably the *double-knits*, which are made on machines with double sets of needles, giving a double thickness to the fabric.

Other weft knits include the *plain jersey*, which can be distinguished by the different direction of the loops on the front and reverse side; the *interlock jersey*, a soft, supple but full-bodied fabric, in which both front and reverse sides have the same appearance; the *rib knits*, which can be recognized by the lengthwise ribs on the back and face of the cloth; the *purl knits*, which show horizontal loops on both sides of the fabric and which have elasticity in the lengthwise direction.

The weft knits can be produced either on circular or flat knitting machines. The circular machines have needles arranged inside a rotating cylinder. They knit the fabric in the form of a tube, which is then cut open and flattened out. Most double-knits are made on circular machines, as are fine- to medium-knit fabrics for dresses, shirts and tailored outerwear, and women's seamless hosiery. Flat knitting machines come in varied forms and are used to produce both the conventional weft knits and many specialty and novelty knits.

The warp-knit fabrics are made only on flat machines. They are generally stronger and more resistant to snag than the weft knits.

The most common form of warp knit is *tricot*, which has fine vertical loops on the face of the fabric and cross-

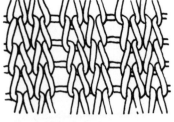

*Jacquard double-knit*

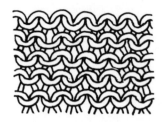

*Purl weft knit*

*2 X 2 rib knit*

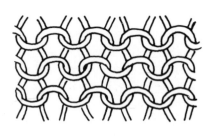

*Single-knit*

*Double-knit*

*Jersey tricot knit*

wise ribs on the back. Major uses of tricot are in lingerie, lining fabrics and blouses.

*Raschel knits* are the other significant form of warp knits. These are lacy, open or patterned knit fabrics which can be produced in an enormous variety of designs by special raschel machines with different attachments.

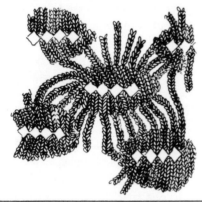

*Ketten raschel knit*

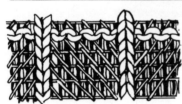

*Tattersall raschel knit*

*Bouclé novelty yarn used in a raschel structure*

*Raschel*

## Every Fabric Has Its Purpose

Someday we may have a single all-purpose fiber to provide us with fabrics that gleam and drape like silk, absorb perspiration like cotton or rayon but wash like polyester, are warm and rich like a quality wool or cool and light as a fine linen, can be made into bulky knits or fine wovens, can be permanently pressed by simple home processes, cleaned of all stains by machine washing, never need ironing and last a lifetime. Until that day of perfection, however, we are going to be using many different fibers and fabrics to meet different clothing needs. In home sewing it is particularly important that you pick the fabric most suitable to the purpose you have in mind.

Every fiber has its virtues and its faults, and they both derive from the nature of the fiber. Nylons, polyesters and acrylics wash easily without much wrinkling and dry rapidly because they do not readily absorb moisture. But the same trait can make a tightly woven synthetic hot and uncomfortable in summer because it doesn't absorb perspiration. Cotton and rayon are highly moisture-absorbent and thus comfortable to wear, but their dimensional stability—ability to retain shape and size when cleaned or worn—is only fair to poor unless they are specially treated. Man-made fibers are "thermoplastic"—they can be set into permanent pleats by heat and chemical treatment—but too hot a dryer may, in reverse, take the pleats out. Silk and wool take the most brilliant of colors, but they usually can't be washed.

Modern textile technology has emphasized many of the virtues and eliminated or diminished some of the faults through blends, combinations and special finishes. In a polyester-cotton blend, for example, the cotton fibers contribute softness and absorbency while the harsher polyester fibers give the fabric dimensional stability and wash-and-wear properties. Acrylics lend warmth and wool-like softness to a blend, acetates can contribute luster and drapeability, nylon adds strength.

Generally the most significant properties of the fabric will be those of the dominant fiber in the blend or combination. A rule of thumb is that a textile should contain at least 50 percent of the fiber whose characteristics are the more important. There are some exceptions, however. For instance, less than 10 percent spandex or anidex in a blended or combination fabric will give it excellent stretch properties.

Government labeling regulations will help you determine what fibers are in the fabric you are buying.

# ✤IV
## *Know What You're Buying*

The large number of [textile] products on the market, each with different care performance, has made it almost impossible for consumers to be informed about any one product, much less the entire range. The traditional source of care information, personal experience by trial and error, no longer meets the needs of consumers.

> —Federal Trade Commission,
> 1972

The most knowledgeable people have trouble identifying the fabric of which a garment is made, and even when given this information they cannot adequately predict the garment's performance. . . . As a rule the sales clerk is just as confused as the customer. . . .

> —Report to the President's
> Committee on Consumer Interests,
> prepared by Consumers Union,
> 1966

In July, 1972, the Federal Trade Commission put into effect two new regulations concerning labeling of both finished garments and fabrics sold by the yard which, if successfully enforced, will have the most significant impact of any such rules ever promulgated.

The first laid down specific rules for the *permanent* labeling of most manufactured clothes and yard goods with absolutely clear instructions for cleaning, drying and ironing. The second prescribed strict standards of nonflammability for children's sleepwear in sizes up to 6X and, for an interim period, the identification by label of all such garments that did not meet those standards. All children's sleepwear in sizes up to 6X manufactured after July 30, 1973, *must* meet the nonflammability standards.

Together with earlier legislation requiring identification of the fiber content of all fabrics and, in the case of wool, a description of the type of wool, the new regulations should help to take a good part of the mystery out of the identification of fabrics and the care of clothes.

The main provisions of the fiber identification and care labeling laws are outlined here, so that you will know your rights as a consumer. In the case of yard goods particularly, it is impossible for the Federal Trade Commission to police every store every day of the week and the enforcement of care labeling is part of the responsibility of every woman who sews.

## Care Labeling Regulations

The Federal Trade Commission has summarized the new care labeling regulations in an excellent Fact Sheet. Its text (with some author's comments) follows:

The Trade Regulation Rule requires that most articles of wearing apparel bear permanent CARE LABELS and that permanent CARE LABELS be supplied with most fabrics bought to make clothes. The first-stage rule affects most domestic and imported apparel and fabrics finished on or after July 3, 1972. Additional product categories may be added by the Commission after 18 months.

ITEMS COVERED: Finished textile garments requiring care and maintenance for ordinary use; textile piece goods consumers use to make apparel.

ITEMS NOT COVERED: Hosiery (except some sheer hosiery products and those that color bleed, which must have care labels); headwear, handwear and footwear; items that need no maintenance; completely washable items intended to retail for $3 or less, if the FTC exempts them on petition; fur and leather items; purely decorative and ornamental items; see-through or other items that would be substantially impaired by a care label, if the FTC exempts them on petition; remnants cut and shipped by the manufacturer, commonly known as "mill ends."

(*Author's note:* The last item has aroused some controversy. As defined by the FTC, "mill ends" mean remnants of ten yards or less which are received by the retail store in that condition. Many retail shops buy piece goods in this form. If you see a remnant, your best bet is to ask the retailer if he has the same fabric on a bolt. If he has, he is required to supply you with a label containing care instructions.)

PERMANENT CARE LABELS must disclose fully, clearly and thoroughly *regular* care and maintenance required by the mere use of the product. Spot care information is *not* required.

*The labels must: inform* how to wash, iron, dry, bleach dryclean and do any other procedures regularly used to maintain or care for a particular article; *warn* if usual care methods seem to apply, but do not; *stay attached* and legible for the life of the garment; *be easy to locate* on apparel and visible on packaged items —or the package itself must repeat the instructions; *use words and phrases,* not symbols; *apply to all components* of the product—any exceptions must be indicated on the label.

*The labels must not: use promotional language*—"Never needs ironing" does not disclose whether ironing is possible, and at what temperature; *omit warning against drycleaning* if the garment cannot be dry-cleaned—consumers are entitled to assume that a garment labeled only with laundering instructions is also drycleanable, in the absence of warning language. Examples: "Do not dryclean," "Machine Wash Only"; *omit positive instructions*—"No Bleach" does not tell what to do; "Dryclean" may be insufficient; unless "dryclean" is based on a test with a chlorinated solvent additional words must be used, such as "Dryclean in petroleum solvents."

CONSUMERS RIGHTS AND RESPONSIBILITIES: *When they shop*—use care labels to predict performance and cost of upkeep in choosing which items to buy; expect salespersons at fabric counters to provide care labels suitable for application to each finished garment. *When they sew*—attach care labels to garments. *In washing, ironing and drycleaning*—follow care label instructions; observe solvent warnings when using coin-operated cleaning equipment; observe warning to professional dryclean only; expect commercial drycleaners to observe care labels. *In speaking up*—share with the FTC ideas to improve care labeling; complain to store managers if rule appears to be violated, obtain name of manufacturer and complain in writing; complain to manufacturers if care instructions are confusing or appear to result in damage to garment.

INDUSTRY RESPONSIBILITIES: The person or organization that directed or controlled the manufacture of the finished article is responsible for *care labeling of apparel.* In most cases, this will be the finished product manufacturer. However, in some situations responsibility may rest with jobbers or retailers. The manufacturer of *piece goods* is responsible for supplying retailers with enough labels to satisfy individual consumers. Retailers are responsible for making such *labels available at point of sale.* The importer is responsible for seeing that imported items are properly labeled before they are sold in commerce.

## What Is the Fabric Made of?

Federal Trade Commission regulations—issued under the Textile Fiber Products Identification Act and the Wool Products Labeling Act—also require that apparel and household textile products (with certain exceptions) must carry conspicuous and securely attached labels identifying the fiber content of the fabric.

The information that must appear on the label, according to an FTC handbook:

must set forth the name of the manufacturer or other

person marketing the textile fiber product or the registered identification number assigned by the Commission to such firm. Also, the label is required to show the generic names and percentages of all fibers in the product in amounts of 5% or more listed in order of predominance by weight. Fibers present to the extent of less than 5% should be disclosed as "other fiber" or "other fibers," as the case may be, and not by their generic names or fiber trademark. The only exception would be where such fibers have a definite functional significance which is clearly stated, as for example "96% acetate 4% spandex for elasticity." If the textile fiber product has been imported the label must show the name of the country where processed or manufactured.

Unfortunately for the fabric shopper, "remnants" do not have to be labeled with the specific fiber content. The retailer may label them individually with a designation "remnant of undetermined fiber content" or he may display a collection of remnants under a *conspicuous* sign with the same designation. If the remnants are all of the same fiber content, they may be displayed under a sign that says, for example, "remnants, 100 percent cotton" or "remnants, 50 percent rayon, 50 percent acetate," etc.

My advice is that if you can't get a care label for the piece of goods you are buying or an identification of its content, you would be better off looking for something else. Or if you see an "undetermined content" remnant, ask if the shop has the same fabric on a bolt, in which case it will be labeled.

The Federal Trade Commission has issued a booklet containing 106 questions and answers about the product identification regulations, which is obtainable by writing to the FTC, Division of Textiles and Furs, in Washington, D.C. In addition to the main provisions noted above, some others of interest include:

• The fiber content label may be put on the package, if the items in the package are customarily not sold separately.

• If the term "virgin" or "new" is used, the fabric has to be made of fibers never before used in a manufactured product.

• If a product contains, say, 92 percent cotton, 4 percent nylon and 4 percent rayon, it should be labeled "92 percent cotton, 8 percent other fibers" because the noncotton fibers are each less than 5 percent of the total.

• A product made entirely of linen must be labeled "100 percent linen" or "all linen."

• The generic name of the fiber (see Chapter III) must be used, although *nondeceptive* terms that truly describe the fiber—for example, "100 percent *combed* cotton" or "100 percent *solution-dyed* acetate"—may be added. The fiber's trademarked name, say "Orlon" or "Acrilan," may also be used, but *only* in conjunction with the generic name—e.g., "Orlon acrylic," or "Acrilan acrylic."

Apparel and yard goods made wholly or partly of wool are covered under the Wool Products Labeling Act. (Wool carpets, rugs and upholstery material come under the Textile Fiber Products Identification Act.) The information required on the label is spelled out as follows by the FTC:

The label or other means of identification affixed

to a wool product should show not only the percentage of wool, reprocessed wool, reused wool, but that of other fibers as well, and in addition an identifying name or registered identification number which may be that of the manufacturer or that of a person or firm marketing the product in interstate commerce. Fibers present to the extent of less than 5% should be disclosed as "other fiber" or "other fibers," as the case may be, and not by their generic name or fiber trademark. The only exception would be where such fibers have a definite functional significance which is clearly stated in connection with the disclosure, as for example "96% wool, 4% spandex for elasticity."

The term *wool*, as defined by the Act, is "the fiber from the fleece of the sheep or lamb or hair of the Angora or Cashmere goat (and may include the so-called specialty fibers from the hair of the camel, alpaca, llama and vicuna) which has never been reclaimed from any woven or felted wool product." [See Chapter VI for definitions of "virgin wool," "reprocessed wool," etc.]

## Flammability Labeling

In 1954, Congress passed the Flammable Fabrics Act (amended in 1967) whose stated purpose was "to prohibit the introduction or movement in interstate commerce of articles of wearing apparel and fabrics which are so highly flammable as to be dangerous when worn by individuals and for other purposes." The Federal Trade Commission issued a series of regulations to implement the act, setting standards of flammability and procedures for the testing of fabrics.

Unhappily, despite its good intentions, the act didn't work too well, the standards and test procedures were too loose and enforcement was too complex and difficult. The extremely dangerous flammability of children's sleepwear, in particular, caused mounting concern. So in July, 1972, the Federal Trade Commission put into effect new standards for children's sleepwear and new sampling procedures to make sure that all fabrics involved were tested at close enough intervals to ensure that no substantial yardage would be missed. It also introduced, on an interim basis until all manufacturers could meet the new standards, so-called negative labeling, which is probably one of the best ways yet devised to ensure compliance.

Under the negative labeling provision every piece of children's sleepwear—nightgowns, pajamas, robes, etc.—and "any fabric or related material intended or promoted for use in children's sleepwear" manufactured after July 30, 1972, that did not meet the standards had to carry a label reading: *"Flammable (Does Not Meet U.S. Department of Commerce Standard DOC FF 3-71)/Should Not Be Worn Near Sources of Fire."* Flammable sleepwear was required to carry such a label until July 30, 1973—at which date *all* sleepwear in the specified sizes had to comply with the standards, or be taken off the market.

In addition, all items of children's sleepwear up to size 6X must carry a care label, permanently attached to the garment, with precautionary instructions to protect the items from "agents or treatments which are known to cause deterioration of their flame resistance." If the item has been originally tested after one washing and drying, it must be labeled with instructions to wash before wearing.

The new regulations spurred immediate action by both the fiber-making companies and the textile firms to develop fabrics that would meet the new standards. At this writing the outlook is for further regulations that will expand the areas covered to children's sleepwear in the larger sizes.

# V

## Cotton–The King of Natural Fabrics

IN HOME SEWING, cotton was always the "beginner's fabric." It is the easiest cloth to sew, can provide gratifying results and is generally inexpensive. Though cotton is still the ideal fabric to start with, the cottons you will find in retail fabric shops today also include expensive imported prints for summer or resort evening wear, gossamer knits that feel like silk, and fine lawn Liberty prints that are almost irresistible.

Cotton is a natural cellulose fiber that comes from the boll of the cotton plant. It is the number-one fiber in the world for countless apparel, household and industrial purposes, although in the United States its production was passed by the man-made fibers in the 1960s.

Cotton's place in the world of fabrics is due to a number of good properties including softness, light weight and an ability to absorb and evaporate body moisture, which makes it very comfortable to wear. It launders easily and accepts dyeing well. However, unless it is specially treated or blended with synthetics, cotton lacks wash-and-wear properties, wrinkles in wearing and requires considerable ironing.

## The Machines That Made History

The history of cotton is tied in with that of civilizations and nations—not least, the United States. It has given us fabrics that evoke varied images—gingham, flannel, organdy, dotted swiss, denim.

Traces of the cotton plant go back to prehistoric times. According to archeological findings, use of cotton as a fabric dates back at least four or five thousand years in Peru and what is today Pakistan. In more modern times, the invention of machines connected with the plant's cultivation and production of the fabric created historical impacts as great in their day as the discovery of penicillin or man's landing on the moon in ours.

In the American colonies, cotton was one of the earliest crops cultivated in Virginia. At about the same time, British and Dutch "East India" companies were beginning to bring cotton from the Orient to the West. In the early 1640s, Manchester, England, was manufacturing dimities and other cotton fabrics.

In the 1700s, the modern textile industry was born. Inventions followed one another to advance the industry in great forward leaps. In 1730, the first cotton yarn was spun by machine in England. A few years later John Kay invented the *flying shuttle*, which carried the horizontal threads (weft) in weaving swiftly across the loom, increasing the production of a loom fourfold. In the 1760s, the *spinning jenny* made possible the automatic production of cotton yarn. Then Richard Arkwright, sometimes called "the father of the modern textile industry," developed a method of harnessing devices for high-speed spinning of cotton yarn to water power. In the 1780s, the first power-operated loom was developed.

It was an American, Eli Whitney, whose invention in 1793 was to revolutionize the production of cotton. This was the *cotton gin*, which mechanically separated the cotton fiber, or lint, from the seed. Before the gin, this was slow, tedious work because the lint and seed cling tightly together and separating a pound of lint was a day's work for a man. With the cotton gin, the output was increased to fifty pounds a day per man.

These beginnings were followed by great improvements over the years in the cotton seed and, accordingly, in the quality of the fabric; by the development of extremely high-speed automatic spinning and weaving machines; by the discovery of such processes as mercerizing, which adds strength, luster and greater dyeing capabilities, the "Sanforized" process, which controls shrinkage, and more recently durable press, which reduces or eliminates ironing.

One of the most significant advances in the modern cotton fabric was the blending of cotton with synthetics, especially polyester. To the softness and absorbency of cotton, polyester adds true wash-and-wear qualities, better wrinkle resistance and pleat retention.

## How Cotton Is Made

When it bursts open at maturity, the boll of each cotton plant contains about a million fibers—tiny tubes that have grown from cells in the wall of the newly formed seed. Each fiber is filled with layers of cellulose in a spiral form. This complicated structure gives the cotton its strength and absorbency.

Besides the fiber, the cotton plant supplies a fuzz called "linters" which surrounds the seed and is used in producing some rayons and acetates; the seed hulls, which are used for cattle feed; and seed meat, which is made into cottonseed oil.

Picked off the bolls by mechanical harvesting machines, the cotton is trucked to the gin—descendant of Eli Whitney's eighteenth-century machine—where it is cleaned of twigs, leaf trash, dirt and other foreign matter. In the gin "stand," the fibers, or lint, are separated from the seed and each goes its separate way—the lint to make fabrics, the seeds and their linter fuzz to be manufactured into oil, feedstuffs and other products.

After ginning, the cotton is baled and each bale is classified according to (1) length of staple, (2) grade and (3) character. These determine the value of the cotton. Different varieties of cotton will produce different staple lengths. The average length of the cotton fiber is about one and a half inches. Longer fibers are considered superior because they produce a silkier fabric. Grades of cotton are established in the United States by the government according to color, amount of foreign matter and ginning preparation. Character takes into account those properties of the fiber —strength, smoothness, uniformity, maturity—not covered by the staple and grade definitions.

The cottons usually considered the highest in quality are the Sea Island, Egyptian and "Supima" types. These are most often used in highly-styled fabrics and are not blended with synthetics.

In the spinning of cotton yarn, the fiber is processed in various ways. One of them is *carding*, a method of further cleaning the fibers, rearranging them and forming a "sliver," a ropelike strand about the thickness of a finger. All fine cottons must also be *combed;* this removes the shorter fibers and produces a smooth, silky strong yarn.

When the yarn is ready for weaving, it goes on high-speed looms to be manufactured into one of three basic woven patterns—plain, twill and satin (described in Chapter III). Some cotton mills do everything in the manufacture of the textile—spin, weave, dye and finish. Others sell unfinished greige goods to converters, to be finished in a variety of ways.

## The Principal Cotton Finishes

Some of the finishes that are meaningful to the consumer are:

• *Mercerizing*, a process that gives a fabric the lustrous and silky appearance found in fine cottons and also improves its strength and dyeability.

• *Compressive shrinkage*, which reduces the amount of shrinkage in the finished fabric, usually to less than 2 percent. Most familiar in this area is the trademark "Sanforized."

• *Mechanical processing*, to emboss, nap or otherwise change the surface appearance of the fabric (from flannel to moiré).

• *Chemical processing*, to add such properties to the cotton fabric as wash-and-wear, fire resistance, stain resistance and controlled shrinkage.

# The Cotton Knits

In addition to its larger use in woven fabrics, cotton can also be knitted on circular, warp (flat) or raschel machines to produce varied types of knit cloths. Until recent years cotton knits were used mainly in underwear, T-shirts and active sportswear. Constant improvements in knitting and finishing techniques, particularly in Europe, have made it possible to use these knits in couture designs. The importing firm of Fisba, Inc., for example, has a cotton knit of gossamer weight that has the usual opaqueness of cotton combined with a silklike hand. Of course, this fabric has a price to match its quality, but just running my fingers over the surface made me feel that this was a cloth I must have.

# Names for Cotton Fabrics

Many cotton fabrics have identifying type names. In some cases (for example, where the name identifies a particular weave), these names may also be applied to other cloths. The most widely known include:

*Batiste*: a lightweight fabric, semi-opaque, with a crisp hand.

*Broadcloth*: smooth, with a plain weave, the basis for many printed cotton fabrics.

*Chambray*: cotton fabric with a heather color effect, used in light shirtings.

*Chintz*: cotton with a shining surface, usually printed, used a great deal in draperies and slipcovers.

*Cord*: fabric with a raised ribbing and firm body, excellent in suits and sportswear.

*Corduroy*: cloth with a napped and ridged velvety surface.

*Denim*: a tough fabric made famous by blue jeans, highly fashionable today.

*Dimity*: a crisp, semi-sheer fabric, usually printed.

*Dotted Swiss*: a sheer fabric with raised tufts scattered on the surface.

*Duck*: a canvas-type fabric used for sportswear.

*Flannel*: in cotton, this is everybody's favorite nightgown.

*Gingham*: one of cotton's most famous fabrics; various types of woven checks in two tones, one of them usually white.

*Lace*: an open, crochet-type cotton lace.

*Lawn*: a soft, semi-sheer fabric, usually printed.

*Organdy*: crisp and transparent, popular for household use (e.g., curtains) as well as apparel.

*Oxford*: a shirting material, usually in white or solid colors.

*Piqué*: a waffle-type weave, crisp and most popular in white.

*Plissé*: a puckered fabric in which the puckering is mechanically embossed.

*Poplin*: tightly woven twill with a firm hand, for sportswear.

*Sateen*: a satin weave whose luster has been mechanically increased, usually printed for apparel use.

*Seersucker*: puckered cloth in which the puckering is done in the weaving.

*Shirting*: a name given to woven fabrics used in shirts, including broadcloth, oxford and chambray.

*Terry*: a looped cloth used in towels and beachwear.

*Velveteen*: a napped, velvet-type surface similar to corduroy but without ribbing.

*Voile*: a sheer fabric, more transparent than batiste but with the same crisp hand.

## Light and Heavy Weights

The word "ply" is used to define the number of strands in the yarn. In the woven fabrics, cotton comes in lightweight single-ply—gingham, broadcloth, sateen, etc.—for summer garments, and in a heavier two-ply construction for suits and sportswear.

Most of the lightweight cottons are now available blended with polyester, and if the practical care aspects of the fabric are most important, these blends are recommended over all-cotton fabrics.

There are, however, old-fashioned cottons that the inspired home designer can tailor into garments with great charm, such as chintz, dimity and dotted swiss. These are largely all-cotton, especially if they are imported. All-cotton imports also include fine fabrics from France and Italy which are often screen printed in rich colors and are sometimes difficult to tell from silk. The cotton Liberty prints from England, small floral patterns on very fine lawn, are especially charming.

In the very high grade cottons, the threads may be so fine that a two-ply yarn can be used in a fabric as sheer as voile to give it greater strength. This construction is found mainly in imported cottons.

In the two-ply and heavier cloths, the advantages of polyester blends are not as significant an in the single-ply fabrics. For one thing, the heavier weight helps the cloth keep its original shape. Also, since the all-cotton is more moisture-absorbent than the cotton-polyester blend, it is more comfortable in hot weather.

## Sewing with Cotton

All lightweight cottons can be sewn with a size 11 needle (ballpoint for knits). A thicker needle, size 14, is suitable for the heavier fabrics. Stitches should be spaced between 10 and 15 to the inch, depending on the weight of the fabric (the heavier fabrics require the smaller number). Moderate tension should be used for wovens and a loose tension for knits. Experimenting with scraps will help.

In ironing cotton, pressing with a dry iron on a dampened cloth placed over the fabric or garment is superior to steam pressing. When sewing, the wrong side of the fabric should be pressed. When ironing a finished garment, press on the right side. All-cotton takes a higher ironing heat than cotton-synthetic blends. The latter must be ironed at a temperature setting no higher than that permissible for the synthetic in the blend. If you're uncertain about the fiber content, test a scrap of the material or an inconspicuous part of the garment. Always begin with a light ironing pressure on cotton and cotton blends, increasing the pressure gradually as required.

## The Care of Cotton Clothes

Make sure you read the instructions that should come with the bolt of fabric or manufactured garment. Cottons blended with synthetics must be washed, machine-dried and ironed at lower temperatures than all-cotton.

All-cotton can be washed in hot water; in fact, it can be boiled if sterilization is required, as with diapers. Today's dyes are colorfast, with the exception of madras and some ethnic cloths, but it is better to wash lights and darks separately. Cotton can take bleaching when necessary; a chlorine bleach, however, may cause some finishes to yellow.

Cotton clothes will iron best when slightly damp and can be pressed either on the wrong side or on the right side with a damp cloth. This, of course, means a dry, not a steam, iron.

Cottons can be dry cleaned, but this should be reserved for garments too complicated to wash comfortably as dry cleaning sometimes tends to yellow and diminish the sparkle in the fabric.

## Some Wholesale Resources

The following wholesale resources—textile companies, converters and importers—are among those that sell to retail fabric shops and will be able to supply your favorite store if it is out of the type of cottons they handle. Many of their fabrics are blended with polyester for easy care.

*Bates Company, 1412 Broadway, New York City:* Cotton prints, embroideries, novelties.

*Boussac of France, 1412 Broadway, New York City:* Beautiful French cottons.

*Concord Fabrics, 1411 Broadway, New York City:* Very large selection of tailored cottons, knit and woven.

*Cone Mills, Inc., 1440 Broadway, New York City:* Denims, corduroys, prints; large selection.

*Crompton-Richmond, 1071 Avenue of the Americas, New York City:* Corduroys, velveteens, printed and plain.

*Dan River Mills, 111 West 40th Street, New York City:* Wide selection of quilts, knits, fancies and ginghams.

*Fisba, Inc., 1457 Broadway, New York City:* Very high quality Swiss cotton prints, knits and wovens.

*Henry Glass and Company, 1071 Avenue of the Americas, New York City:* Cotton prints, sheers, quilted.

*Jos. Goldinger Company, Inc., 36 West 37th Street, New York City:* Imported Japanese screen prints on cottons; others.

*Spring Mills, 1430 Broadway, New York City:* Cottons and novelties, also "ultrasuede."

*Troy Textiles, 1412 Broadway, New York City:* Cottons, blends, quilted.

# VI
## Wool–The Air-Conditioned Fabric

THE ORIGIN OF wool goes back to prehistoric times when, by some process unknown to us, man found he could clip the fleece of sheep and spin and weave it into cloth. According to a fourteenth-century couplet, Mother Eve was the first wool processor: "When Adam delved and Eve span/Who was then the gentleman?" Wool and sheep are part of man's mythology, his biblical history, his nursery rhymes and fairy tales and, not least, of the mercantile growth of nations and empires.

Wool is the second most popular of the natural fibers, after cotton. In the forty years from 1930 to 1970, world production of wool fibers increased by about one-third to more than three billion pounds. In the United States, however, there has been a steady decline in the use of wool (as well as cotton) since production of the synthetics spurted sharply in the 1960s. In 1960, American textile mills used 480 million pounds of wool fibers; this was 7.5 percent of all fibers, natural and synthetic, processed in the United States. By 1970, this had fallen to 273.3 million pounds, or only 3 percent of all fibers. Whether this trend will be reversed remains to be seen, but as noted in a previous chapter, there has been a noticeable reawakening of interest among American women in the natural cloths.

The fleece of sheep, and certain goats, used in making wool fabrics consists of staple fibers of varied lengths. Different breeds of sheep provide different types of fleece, from very fine to coarse.

The fleece is usually sheared from the sheep before warm weather sets in by skilled teams of shearers who travel to the individual ranches for this purpose. The shorn fleece is packed in bags of about 250 pounds, each bag representing the contribution of approximately twenty-five sheep. When the bags reach the mills, the wool is sorted and graded according to the fiber diameter, which will vary from breed to breed. This classification insures that the fiber will go into the fabric it is best suited for.

Next comes the scouring, or washing, of the wool, which contains a large amount of dirt, grease and other foreign matter. The wool is dried by hot air, preparing it for the next processing stages.

*Carding* is the process of untangling the fibers which have become closely wound together in the washing and sorting of the wool. This is done by carding cylinders which are covered with wire teeth that arrange the fibers more or less parallel with one another and clean out extraneous matter.

## Woolens and Worsteds

There are two basic types of wool: *woolen* and *worsted*. Woolens are produced by spinning the fibers into yarn

*Woolen yarn*

*Worsted yarn*

after carding; the yarn is characterized by a soft, slightly hairy surface. The worsted yarn is further processed by combing after carding. This removes the shorter fibers and produces a tighter, smoother yarn with a dry, crisp hand. If you compare the feel of a bulky woolen sweater with the feel of worsted gabardine cloth you can readily tell the difference between the two types of wool.

## The Characteristics of Wool

Wool has a number of inherent characteristics that are highly desirable in apparel. The fiber has a natural three-dimensional crimp, or spiral twist, which is sometimes given to synthetics by mechanical or chemical processing. When wool is stretched, the fibers tend to return to their original position. This resiliency means that a good wool garment doesn't easily wrinkle or lose its shape. In fact, hanging up a dress or suit overnight will usually take out the wrinkles.

Wool can be produced in almost any color because the fibers combine with a great variety of dyes; for richness and brilliance of color it can be matched or surpassed only by silk. Wool is absorbent. In summer, it will absorb perspiration; in winter, it will soak up damp. It insulates from both tropic heat and Arctic cold because the air pockets that form among its crimpy fibers slow down the transfer of heat between the body and the outside air, and vice versa.

The feel of wool is often a good indication of its quality. In the hand, a worsted has a dry crispness and springs back into unwrinkled condition after being rolled up in a fist. A woolen fabric will be soft and yielding when handled, and the finer the quality, the softer it will feel.

Wool can form the sheerest of voiles (often printed) or the thickest of meltons and fleeces. Sometimes it is blended with other fibers. This is done to add to the fabric the appearance or performance of the other fiber, or to reduce the cost of the cloth. When shopping for a wool fabric you should compare the all-wool and the blends to judge which one will suit your purpose best.

## Wovens and Knits

Wool fabrics, both woolens and worsteds, are manufactured in either woven or knit form. Most double-knits are worsted. In the woven fabrics, many patterns such as checks, plaids, and other novelties, are available in both woolens and worsteds. The worsteds will generally be more expensive than the woolens, so if your design does not require a flat crisp look you may want to consider the woolen type.

The knit fabrics come as single-knit, or jersey, and double-knit, which has two layers of stitches knitted together in a single fabric, and is a great material for traveling clothes. All wool knits come in novelty patterns as well as plain.

## To Line or Not to Line

Until the recent upheaval in fashion it was customary to line most garments made of woven wool. Today the trend is to leave most garments unlined for the natural look. But some clothes, jackets and coats, for example, still require linings so they will drape and hold their shape better, and people who are allergic to the fabric need linings in all their woolen garments.

The double-knits do not require linings for shape retention. Single-knits are often lined, but there is a knit called *interlock*, produced by Jasco in this country and by Racine in France, that needs no lining to retain its shape.

New finishing processes in recent years have added some important properties to wool fabrics. Wool has historically been a favorite food of moths because of its protein content. Today manufacturers can add chemicals to the cloth to permanently mothproof it. When you are buying wool check this detail.

Currently federal regulations do not require that special finishes, such as mothproofing and water repellancy, be indicated on labels. However, it is to the manufacturers' advantage to make known to the consumer all the benefits of their fabrics; accordingly, the information may be imprinted somewhere on the bolt or label. If not, the sales person will very likely know if any special finishes have been applied to the goods.

# New or Used?

A label on the bolt must tell you whether the fabric you are buying is new, reprocessed or reused.

Virgin wool, pure wool or 100 percent wool indicates the fiber has never before been manufactured into fabric. If the label specifies 100 percent wool, other fibers may be included for ornamental purposes, but no more than 5 percent.

Reprocessed wool is wool that has been made into cloth and then turned back into fiber without having been worn or used. Usually this comes from mill ends and clippings.

Reused wool is a fabric made of worn or used articles that have been changed back into fiber and then converted again into cloth. The most common example is interfacing for warmth of a winter coat.

# The Variety of Wool Fabrics

Wools come in a great variety of constructions, textures and surface finishes, to the extent that most wool fabrics have individual names and identities. The cloths you are most likely to find in stores are listed below. (See color insert for photographs.) Some of the names are also used for fabrics made of other fibers.

*Bengaline*: a firm, lustrous fabric with heavy cords running horizontally, giving it a striped effect.

*Boucle*: a fabric with a looped or knotted effect texturing the surface, sometimes on both sides.

*Broadcloth*: very smooth, a velvety napped cloth (should be cut one way). The name comes from the method of weaving on a very broad loom. Excellent for dressy clothes.

*Cavalry Twill*: firm fabric with a corded diagonal twill; very sporty.

*Challis*: an almost sheer plain weave worsted, usually printed.

*Chinchilla Cloth*: heavy cloth for overcoats with a deep, nubby, tufted surface. Chinchilla makes up into clothes with a very youthful look and is also popular in children's wear. The name comes from Chinchilla, Spain, where it originated.

*Covert*: tightly woven twill, made of yarn with dark and light strands, producing a two-tone effect. Tailors well. Has a natural water repellency.

*Crepe*: a cloth with a pebbled textured surface. Made in a variety of weights from light to heavy.

*Donegal*: a tweed that originated in Donegal, Ireland, now made in U.S. as well. The surface is scattered with multicolored slubs.

*Double-faced Fabrics:* reversible cloth made by weaving two separate cloths together. Often used in coats without linings.

*Double-knit*: knitted by machine with double sets of needles to make one two-layered cloth. Comes in different weights and is one of the most popular types of wool for dresses and other apparel because of its shape retention. Also used in men's suits.

*Duvetyne*: a quality twill fabric with a short, smooth nap.

*Felt*: a nonwoven fabric produced by pressing the fibers together. For sportswear and trim. Can be a fun fabric.

*Flannel*: smooth woven fabric with a slightly napped surface. Comes in woolen or worsted. Tissue weight used for dresses, heavier weights for suits and coats.

*Fleece*: cloth with a deep nap, very warm and handsome. For coats, but looks elegant in a winter skirt or dress.

*Gabardine*: a firm, hard-finished worsted twill. Used for all types of apparel, including men's wear, depending on weight.

*Harris Tweed*: a trademark name for Scottish virgin wool fabric, hand woven in the Outer Hebrides.

*Heathers*: different colored wool fibers are used in the yarn to produce blended tone in tweeds and other sport fabrics.

*Herringbone*: a twill pattern arranged to resemble the backbone of a fish. For sportswear, coats, suits.

*Homespun*: cloth woven from rough, strong yarns, reminiscent of the pioneers. For casual wear.

*Hopsacking*: similar to homespun, but with more open weave.

*Jacquards*: various designs produced on a jacquard loom to resemble tapestry, with colors usually reversed on back of cloth.

*Jersey*: a supple, plain knit, for dresses and sportswear.

*Lamb's Wool*: wool from lambs under seven months old. Very soft.

*Loden*: a thick, stiff cloth, water repellent, used for sports coats. Originally from the Austrian Tyrol.

*Melton*: a heavy, closely woven fabric, showing no surface weave. Used in winter coats.

*Merino*: high-grade, soft wool from merino sheep. Very successful in double-knits.

*Naked Wool*: a recently invented name for very light, sheer wools for year-round use.

*Nun's Veiling*: challis in certain solid colors, mostly black and navy.

*Ottoman*: heavy fabric with round ribs across width of cloth.

*Raschel*: warp knits made on special machines; great variety of designs and open work.

*Serge*: worsted twill with diagonal ribs showing on both sides of cloth. For suitings, sportswear.

*Sharkskin*: a quality worsted in basket weave or twill suiting.

*Shetland*: a soft, somewhat shaggy fabric made of wool from the Shetland Islands, Scotland. *Shetland-type* fabric has a similar hand but may contain no Shetland wool. For sportswear.

*Tartan*: plaids of Scottish clans in twill or plain weave. Numerous apparel uses. Periodically very fashionable.

*Tweed*: soft but durable fabrics with rough-looking surface. Bits of different-color yarn may be added to the wool before spinning for interest. For casual wear.

*Velour*: a closely woven, velvety napped fabric. Used for coats, winter wear.

*Venetian Cloth*: a heavy type of covert with lustrous finish. Handsome in coats, jackets.

*Whipcord*: a twill with clearly defined diagonal cords. Sturdy, for sportswear.

*Wool Fancies*: all types of highly-styled novelty fabrics that are not covered by other designations.

*Zibeline*: fabric with long nap pressed back against the surface. Usually striped. For coatings.

# Rare and Luxury Wools

There is a special group of wools known for their rarity and luxury. These include cashmere, mohair, camel and alpaca. The reader may not be able to find these in the local retail store because they are expensive and not widely stocked. However, brief descriptions are included here.

*Cashmere*: a fabric manufactured from the very fine hair of the cashmere goat, a domesticated animal found in several parts of Asia. It is noted for its light weight and softness. Fabrics come in all-cashmere or in blends of cashmere and other fibers.

*Camel Cloth*: made from the hair of the camel, domesticated in parts of Africa and Asia. The fabric is napped, warm and soft. Camel also is often combined with other wools.

*Alpaca*: comes from the llamalike animal of the same name which is herded in semi-domesticated flocks in

South America, mostly in Peru and Chile. The alpaca is sheared once a year for its long woolly hair. The resulting fiber is strong and silky with a luxurious hand.

*Mohair*: the hair of the Angora goat, which takes its name from the Turkish province where it has been raised for centuries. Today most mohair used in the United States is produced in Texas where Angora goats were introduced more than a hundred years ago. Mohair has a beautiful, silklike hand and is often blended with other fibers, both natural and synthetic.

One other luxury wool is mentioned here only for reference. That is *vicuna*, from the South American animal of the same name which is on the endangered species list; the wool may no longer be imported into the United States.

## Some Tips on Sewing with Wool Fabrics

Wool sold by the yard usually comes preshrunk, ready for the needle. The fabric should have a tag or label to that effect. If it doesn't, the best thing to do is to take it to your dry cleaner and have him steam-press the cloth. Preshrinking can also be done at home with a steam iron and some patience, but using a wet cloth and a dry iron may leave unequally shrunk areas which can become problems later on. Double-knits require no preshrinking.

All knits, double or single, should be laid flat on a table overnight before cutting. Spread the fabric out softly so that it isn't pulled anywhere, and don't let any hang over the edge of the table. Single-knits are suitable for shirred or draped styles, while double-knits make up well into tailored clothes. For both types, use tapes in the shoulder seams, waistlines and necklines to keep the fabric from stretching. Woven interfacings are desirable; these should be of lighter weight than the top fabric. Use a ballpoint needle and silk or nylon thread. Let the garment hang overnight before finishing the hem.

For wovens, be sure your pattern is laid out on the grain of the material. By pulling out a thread across the width of the fabric you can get a straight edge. Steam-press every seam when stitched—first closed, then open. Interface collars and closings where there are buttonholes. Press the hem softly to avoid a sharp edge.

## The Care of Wool Clothes

Some wools are washable, but most will have to be dry cleaned. If the label on the bolt of cloth says the wool is washable, it will also give instructions which should be carefully followed. Spots must be blotted up as quickly as possible. Use either a damp cloth that has been dipped in a mixture of mild soap and cool water or a cleaning fluid, depending on the nature of the spot. On light-colored wools, cover grease spots with talcum powder, leave overnight and then brush off the powder. Avoid hard rubbing or you may mat the wool.

## Some Wholesale Resources

The following is a list of major mills, converters and wholesalers that sell wool fabrics to retail stores.

*Anglo Fabrics, Inc., 1407 Broadway, New York City*: Large variety of wools and wool blends, both basic and novelties. Suit and coating weight plaids, tweeds, blanket plaids—brushed and unbrushed.

*Auburn Fabrics, Inc., 215 West 40th Street, New York City*: Best known for printed wool challis. Novelties include wool blended with silk and mohair. Unique patterns.

*Bellaine Fabrics Inc., 225 West 34th Street, New York City*: Domestic wools, novelty and basic. Also unusual brushed blanket plaids.

*Berlin Woolens, Inc., 247 West 38th Street, New York City*: Wool and wool blends, Donegal tweeds, heather-weave coordinates, popularly priced tartans, classics.

*Burlington Woolens, 1345 Avenue of the Americas, New York City*: Very large group of novelty wools and classics, tweeds, heathers, Donegals, tartans, flannels and others. Warp knits in coating and suit weights. Brushed-wool mohairs.

*Carletex Corporation, 1451 Broadway, New York City*: Washable wools and wool blends, tartans, classics and fancies.

*S. Chaikowitz, Inc., 250 West 39th Street, New York City*: Camel, cashmere and other fine coatings and suitings. Fine imports from Europe.

*Crestwood Fabrics, Inc. 151 West 40th Street, New York City*: Moderately priced wools, mainly solids.

*Eininger-Feuer Textiles, Inc., 1412 Broadway, New York City*: Solid wools and coordinated novelties.

*Fisba, Inc., 1457 Broadway, New York City*: Lightweight wools, voile and challis prints—all imports from Europe. High quality.

*Franetta Fabrics, 151 West 40th Street, New York City*: Mainly mohairs. Wide color range.

*Jasco Fabrics, 450 Seventh Avenue, New York City*: Famous for its interlock jersey, other knits.

*Milbank, Hardy and Minnes, Inc., 9 East 37th Street, New York City*: Imports, mainly British, including complete group of authentic tartans. Also many wash-and-wear wools, high-fashion women's apparel fabrics and men's wear fabrics.

*Pendleton Woolen Mills, 475 Fifth Avenue, New York City*: Plaids and coordinated solids.

*Stetson Woolen Mills, 1440 Broadway, New York City*: Washable wools in flannels and fancies. Camels and cashmeres.

*J. P. Stevens and Company, Inc., 1185 Avenue of the Americas, New York City*: A very large variety of wools and blends, including washable wools. Makers of Hockanum and Forstmann wools.

*Arthur Zeiler Woolens, Inc., 242 West 39th Street, New York City*: Extensive selection of dress, coat and suit weight wools. Camel cloth and cashmere.

# ⚜VII
## *Silk for Luxury*

THE NAME "SILK" evokes images of fabled Oriental caravans and princesses luxuriously gowned. Life is more prosaic today, but the richness and beauty of silk remain.

Originally produced by the industrious silkworm in China, the fiber has enhanced the lavishness of dress through the ages with the most beautiful fabrics the world has ever known in terms of color, luster, their feel against the body and their flow in a garment. But these most luxurious of all fabrics are also the most difficult to take care of, are among the most expensive of all textiles and must be sewn with great care. For today's woman, these factors place silk strictly in the luxury class.

The passionate emotions that silk has aroused over the centuries are visible in any major museum. The shimmer of blue silk covering Sacred Love in Titian's "Sacred and Profane Love" is but one example of how this fabric touched the great artists of the Renaissance.

The recorded history of silk goes back almost five thousand years and the legends are more numerous than facts, but several facts, even if they, too, sound legendary, can be stated with some sureness.

China, which developed sericulture (from the Latin *sericum*, silk) sometime in the twenty-seventh century B.C., guarded her silk industry with great concern for nearly three thousand years, determined to keep the silkworm within her own boundaries. From about 200 B.C., however, finished silk fabrics began to be sent throughout the known world. From China, camel caravans crossed the Gobi Desert and traveled through Samarkand and Bokhara to Baghdad and Damascus, where the silk was sent on to the ruling centers of Europe.

Sometime around 300 A.D. Japan began to cultivate silk and about 250 years later the Emperor Justinian started silk culture in Constantinople. The story is that two Persian monks smuggled silkmoth eggs out of China for him.

## How Silk Is Produced

Since the silkworm is still the sole producer of silk, the initial stages of production haven't changed over the centuries. The silkmoth bred in captivity deposits several hundred tiny eggs, which are put into cold storage until early spring when the mulberry trees begin to leaf. Then the eggs are hatched in the form of small worms. For about six weeks these worms are fed finely chopped mulberry leaves, which they consume almost continuously, growing to seventy times their original size. When they stop eating, their special silk glands (each worm has two) are filled with the fiber-making substance. They are now placed on or climb onto frames and boards prepared for them. Here the worms begin to spin the silk fibers as a cocoon, which in nature is designed to protect the worm until it turns into a chrysalis, then a moth. Moving its head from side to side, the silkworm exudes from an opening near its mouth a continuous flow of a clear, viscous liquid which solidifies into a fiber as it hits the air. The long filament comes out of the opening—called a spinneret—in a series of figure eights that form the egg-shaped cocoon around the worm. The wall of the cocoon is held together by a gummy substance called sericin which surrounds the fiber. The continuous filament that forms the cocoon is up to a half-mile in length.

After the cocoons are completed, they are gathered together and the worms inside are killed by heat. The only ones not destroyed are those needed, as moths, to breed the next generation. When a moth is allowed to develop, the cocoon is too damaged by its emergence to be of any commercial use.

Before the silk fibers can be removed, the cocoon must be boiled to soften and loosen the gummy sericin. The filaments of a number of cocoons are then reeled together to produce a thread called *raw silk*. The sericin, which had held the cocoon together, now serves to bind the filaments together in the silk thread. The thread is again rewound on large frames to make skeins.

Raw silk is further processed before weaving by twisting several threads together; this is called "throwing." The amount and type of twist depends on the type of fabric to be made from the silk yarn.

Besides raw silk, there is *dupion silk*. This is reeled from cocoons that have become joined together by silkworms during the spinning phase of their life. Because two or more filaments result, tangles and knots are produced and, when reeled, the silk has a nubby look.

*Spun silk* yarn is produced by spinning the waste that results from the reeling processes, usually the coarser covering part and the remains of the cocoon.

*Tussah silk* is made from the cocoons of the wild silk-moth, found mostly in China, and some in India. When in worm stage, these feed mainly on oak leaves and the different diet accounts for the different appearance of the fabric, which has irregular ridges in its texture.

The largest producers of raw silk are China and Japan. Also engaged in sericulture are India, the U.S.S.R., Korea, Italy and several other countries in relatively small amounts. The world production of silk recorded in 1938 was 56,500 metric tons, almost half of which was imported into the United States. In 1971, the latest year for which figures are available, we imported less than 200 tons.

Most of the silk in Western Europe comes from China. The silk we use in the United States comes largely from Korea and Italy. Since trade between China and America, has opened up, imports from China can be expected to grow in the years ahead. It is interesting to note that while researching the silk story for this book, my inquiries to the People's Republic of China were answered directly by the China National Textiles Import and Export Corporation in Peking. Brochures listed the silks (and other fabrics) available for export from China, including crepe, georgette, crepe de Chine, gauze, noil poplins (a lineny-looking silk) and all types of pongees that haven't been seen in this country for a long time.

Japan, which used to be a big exporter of silk, now

consumes more than she produces, and in 1971 imported more than 5,000 metric tons of raw silk. This has created an increase in the price of silk on the world market. The current high consumption of silk in Japan is apparently due to an increased demand for ceremonial kimonos. It seems that nostalgia is not limited to the West.

Silk is woven in the three basic weaves found in other fabrics: plain, twill and satin. Silk is either yarn-dyed, piece-dyed or printed. The fiber posseses a natural luster due to its triangular shape, which reflects light, and this in turn contributes to the brilliance and depth of color of silk fabrics.

The word "denier" originally was used as a unit of weight for silk and came to be associated with sheerness in the public mind. The denier number is the weight of 9,000 meters of a continuous filament fiber in grams. The smaller the denier number, the lighter and sheerer the fiber. At one time 15 denier in nylon meant sheer stockings, and 840 denier nylon was used for tires. Today, because of the variety of synthetic fibers made in filament form, denier has lost meaning in consumer language, and is employed mostly in fiber specifications for industrial use.

Silk fabrics can be treated with a number of finishes, including crease and stain resistance.

Some of the silk names and descriptions follow (Photos can be found in the color insert):

*Brocade*: fabric with raised patterns, often floral.

*Chiffon*: very light, soft and semi-transparent, for dressy clothes.

*Faille*: firm cloth with faint rib, for costumes, dresses.

*Flat crepe*: smooth, flat surface for blouses, dresses.

*Fuji*: Plain weave of spun silk, soft, beautiful and usually washable.

*Georgette*: similar to chiffon, but with a crepe hand.

*Habutae*: soft, light, plain weave, often printed. In solid colors, used in linings of expensive clothes.

*Matelasse*: raised patterns on crepe.

*Organza*: sheer, crisp fabric, with luster, for dressy clothes.

*Pongee*: Light, beige silk, usually washable, of tussah yarn.

*Satin*: smooth lustrous cloth, preferred by brides.

*Shantung*: a popular fabric, made of *dupion*, has a nubby, textured surface.

*Surah*: another name for silk twill. Often printed.

*Taffeta*: famous for its rustle and crisp hand. Also the changeableness of its color.

*Twill*: a basic woven pattern, with diagonal weave, for dresses, scarves, ties.

## Sewing with Silk

In sewing silk, use a very fine needle and silk thread. Pins will leave marks, so use the slimmest you can find, or needles. The pattern should be cut and fitted in muslin first because silk is difficult to alter without leaving marks.

When sewing sheer silks, place a piece of tissue paper under the fabric while stitching, then rip the paper away. Also use tissue paper when cutting a sheer fabric, placing the fabric between two sheets of paper. In ironing, always use a pressing cloth and moderate heat, about 250° F. Always press on the wrong side.

## Watch the Care Labels

Most silk is not washable. Check the care instructions on the label very carefully. If in doubt, don't wash.

Attempts at spot cleaning may leave rings. (Care labels don't have to give spot-cleaning instructions.) The best bet is to send a stained garment immediately to the dry cleaner.

If the garment is washable, use lukewarm water with a mild neutral detergent of the type you use for lingerie. Always wash gently by hand. If you need a bleach (for whites only) use peroxide not chlorine.

## Some Wholesale Resources

The firms listed below sell silk fabrics to retail shops:

*Abraham Silks Company, 108 West 39th Street, New York City:* A prominent French-Swiss converter supplying the couture in Europe; planning to bring a moderate price line to the United States for retail sale.

*Amer-Mill Company, 119 West 40th Street, New York City:* Beautiful printed silks.

*Couleur International Ltd., 1412 Broadway, New York City:* Large line of printed silks.

*Onondaga Silk Company, Inc., 1450 Broadway, New York City:* Largest silk wholesale house in the United States.

# VIII
## Linen–The Coolest Fabric

OF ALL FABRICS, natural or synthetic, linen is the coolest for its weight. This, combined with its crispness of hand and pristine appearance in the fine cloths, has made it in the past a favorite in summer dresses and suits.

Today, however, natural linen is going into eclipse as far as clothes are concerned. One reason is that the plant from which the fiber is derived, the blue-flowered flax plant, must be carefully picked—in Ireland this is done by hand—to preserve the fiber. This makes production slow and expensive compared to other fabrics. Its popularity in table linens and handkerchiefs further reduces the amount available for clothing. In addition, a number of the new synthetics or linen-synthetic blends have been able to imitate the linen look closely. And while these synthetics do not have linen's absorbency and coolness—nor the richness of appearance of high-quality linens—they are less expensive and don't crush as easily.

But if you love natural linen—and many women do—linens by the yard are found both in dress goods stores and upholstery departments.

Linen competes with the other natural fibers—cotton, wool and silk—for the title of being the first to be woven into cloth. There are traces of linen production in Switzerland eight thousand to ten thousand years ago. The linen burial shrouds of Egyptian kings have come down to us through thousands of years. The elaborate crisp ruffs of Elizabethan courtiers were made of linen lace. Linen was the clothing of the ancient Hebrew priesthood in the Temple at Jerusalem. It was worn by Cleopatra and by Charlemagne.

The strength of the flax fiber, its ability to be woven in a wide variety of fabrics, from very fine handkerchief weights to heavy homespun, its superiority to all other fibers in absorbing moisture and conducting heat, made linen for many centuries the leading fabric in the Western world—until Eli Whitney's invention of the cotton gin at the end of the eighteenth century, which introduced a new economic factor, a factor of great importance in the historical development of textiles. Now that it was possible to mass produce cotton fabrics at low cost, cotton rapidly began to displace linen in everyday textile use, although linen maintained its popularity as a fashionable summer fabric as well as in household uses.

## How Linen Is Produced

The common flax plant (*linum usitatissimum*, or "most used of the linacae") has two main varieties. The first is grown for its fibers, generally in temperate areas such as Ireland and Belgium. The second is cultivated for its seed—either in cool and temperate zones such as the northern United States and Canada or in tropical areas such as India and Argentina. The seed is used to produce linseed oil for paints, varnishes, inks and other industrial products.

Unlike the cotton plant, whose fibers are in the boll, the useful fibers of the flax plant are in the wiry stem, just under the skin. This makes it necessary to pull up the plant instead of reaping it, so as to avoid damage to the fibers—a vital factor because it limits mass production.

The bundled flax stems are soaked (retted) to loosen the fiber from the stalk, then dried in the open air in conical bundles and threshed (scutched) to remove the fibers. The fibers are then combed (hackled) to remove the shorter strands from the longer ones. The highest-quality linen is produced from the longer fibers, which are often up to two feet in length. The fibers are processed to increase their strength and uniformity and then spun into the long continuous threads, or yarn, which are used in the weaving of linen cloth. Linen is one fiber that has not been used to any extent in knitted cloths because its fibers are not flexible enough.

The woven fabric is finished in ways similar to cotton. It is bleached and mercerized—to shrink it and give it brilliance—and dyed in fashionable colors. To produce checked and striped fabrics, the yarn is dyed before weaving and the patterns are created in the weaving process. Linen also can be printed in a great variety of designs and colors.

These days, quality linens for apparel use are generally treated to improve crease resistance; without such treatment linen wrinkles and crushes very easily. Many apparel linens also are given durable-press finishing.

Linen comes in a number of weights, from hand-kerchief to upholstery. Properly styled, it can be used in many types of apparel—summer streetwear and sportswear, coats, suits, evening dresses. Linens wash well and are usually colorfast—but be sure to check the care label. The plain colors tend to be quiet and pas-toral, most suitable for the casual look.

## The Imitations

There is a great deal of synthetic linen on the market. A fabric made entirely of linen will be labeled "100 per-cent linen" or "all linen." The least expensive and most widely used synthetic linens are those made of rayon. The nubby surface of these fabrics closely resembles that of natural linen, but the properties are those of rayon, not linen. If the fabric is identified as "rayon linen" it is all rayon; if it is a rayon and linen blend, the percentage of each fiber must be stated. In any case, the manufacturer's care instructions should be closely followed, paying attention to the most sensitive fiber. Generally, rayon linen should be dry cleaned and treated like other two-ply rayons in sewing and care. Rayon linens are frequently found in varied prints and novelty effects and usually are treated for crease resis-tance.

Also available are polyester linens. These are usually more expensive than the rayons, but they are pleatable and washable and have all the other advantages of polyester. Here, too, care label instructions must be fol-lowed.

"Silk linen" is all silk and should be treated in every

way as you would silk. It is a luxury fabric, more expensive than natural linen, which it resembles only in its nubby texture.

# Care of Natural Linen

The following guidelines for stain removal and washing of natural linens are recommended by the Irish Linen Guild:

Given prompt attention, most food stains will disappear from linen with ordinary washing. If you can't treat them right away, sponge with cold water and treat as soon as possible. New presoaks are very effective for most food stains. In any case, stains should be removed, as far as possible, before laundering. Washing or ironing may only set some stains. For the most common stains, the following treatments are recommended:

*Alcoholic beverages (except wine):* Soak stain immediately in cold water, rub with glycerine and, if stain persists, rinse in *white* vinegar for a few seconds. *For wine*, sponge with cold water, rub with liquid detergent or glycerine. Wait fifteen minutes, then rinse. Repeat if necessary.

*Chocolate, gravy, ketchup:* Scrape off excess, soak in cool water or enzyme-active presoak, then treat as for lipstick *(see page 81).*

*Coffee, tea (without cream):* Soak stains overnight in strong *white* vinegar and water, then wash as usual.

*Coffee, tea (with cream):* Rub stain with liquid detergent or glycerine to remove grease. Then proceed as for coffee or tea without cream.

*Egg, meat juice:* Scrape off excess. Apply meat tenderizer to stain, or soak in enzyme-active presoak before laundering. Repeat if necessary.

*Fruit:* Soak in cool water. Bleach with hydrogen peroxide or chlorine bleach (white and colorfast colors only). Never use soap and water first on fruit stains. It may set them. Ironing before stains are completely removed will make matters worse.

*Lipstick:* Sponge with cleaning fluid. Rub glycerine on stain to loosen grease. Apply liquid detergent and let set for ten minutes. Rinse in warm water.

*Mustard:* Apply glycerine to stain, then soap or detergent, before laundering. If stain persists, sponge with rubbing alcohol.

*Scorch:* A cloth dipped in 3 percent peroxide and used as a pressing cloth will remove light scorches. Household bleaches also can be used.

## Laundering and Ironing Linens

Regular linens can be hand-washed or machine-washed. They also may be dry cleaned, especially if the styling is too complicated for home washing and drying, or if the garment is lined. In washing, warm water is generally recommended (although white linens can take very hot water), with mild soap or detergent. A water conditioner is recommended for washing and the first deep rinse; it helps keep the linens brighter. If a dryer is used, always *remove garment when slightly damp.* Too high a dryer setting, or overdrying, may bake in wrinkles.

Iron while damp and press until dry, always finishing on the right side to bring out the linen's natural gloss. Set iron at "high" setting, "medium" for finer fabrics.

Some linens are specially finished for crease resistance or durable press. These must be washed and dried differently than regular linens. They should be washed only in warm water (120° to 140° F.) using a mild soap or detergent, and never bleached or starched. Rinse thoroughly. Tumble-dry in automatic dryer, but time the dryer to leave the garment slightly damp. A light touch-up with a steam iron will bring up the luster of the cloth. If washing by hand, never wring or twist. Drip dry, but do not pin to the washline.

## Sewing with Linen

Linen is easy to sew and a pleasure to tailor into jackets, suits, slacks, dresses and other garments that take unfussy lines.

In sewing, the same instructions should be followed as given for cotton (see page 52). These include using fine needles (size 11) for thin linens and heavier needles (size 14) for the heavier fabrics.

Before cutting, press out all the wrinkles in the fabric, either with a dry iron if the fabric is slightly dampened, or a steam iron if not.

Press all seams as they are made, first closed then open, using either a steam iron or a dry iron and a damp cloth.

For information on wholesale sources of linen, you may refer your retail shop to Hamilton Adams Imports,

Ltd. (24 West 40th Street, New York City), which distributes Irish Moygashel linen in the United States, or the Belgian Linen Association (280 Madison Avenue, New York City), which will supply a list of firms selling upholstery-type Belgian linens.

# IX

## The Cellulosic Fibers—
## Rayons, Acetates, Triacetates

RAYONS, ACETATES AND triacetates are grouped together because they form a family of man-made fibers produced from cellulose, the fibrous substance of all plant life.

### The Rayons

The oldest member of the group is rayon. A French scientist in the late nineteenth century by the name of Count Hilaire de Chardonnet is credited with making the discoveries that eventually produced rayon. Copying the silkworm, he succeeded in extracting cellulose from mulberry leaves and extruding a solution through tiny holes at the end of a nozzle to form fiber filaments. The fabrics he was able to create from these fibers were demonstrated at the 1889 Paris World Exhibition, the same exhibition for which the Eiffel Tower was built.

84

Both created a sensation. This, incidentally, was exactly fifty years before nylon was demonstrated at another World Fair, in New York City. De Chardonnet called his fibers "artificial silk."

Commercially, the fiber didn't become important until our century. It was first produced in the United States in 1910 by American Viscose Company (now the American Viscose Division of FMC Corporation) and took the name "rayon" around 1924.

Because of its low cost as a "dressy" fabric, plus some good apparel properties (it also has some handicaps), rayon became extremely popular and for many years was second only to cotton in world use. More recently its position among the man-made fibers has been seriously challenged by the noncellulosics (nylons, polyesters, acrylics), and in the United States the latest figures indicate that it has been surpassed by these true synthetics. Nonetheless, its inexpensiveness, special qualities and ability to imitate other fabrics give rayon a continuing importance in apparel as well as in other consumer and industrial uses.

Today rayon is made of cellulose derived mainly from wood pulp, which is chemically converted into a soluble compound. This mixture is extruded through a spinneret to form filaments which are regenerated into almost pure cellulose. Since cellulose is natural vegetable matter—only its conversion into fiber is a man-made process—the distinction of being the first true synthetic fiber rests with nylon.

There are a number of types of rayons, distinguished by how the cellulose is processed and regenerated, but their basic properties are similar. These include: a good ability to absorb moisture, which makes it comfortable to wear and receptive to dyes in an almost unlimited range of colors; good colorfastness and drapeability; ability to blend well with many other fibers, both natural and synthetic.

Disadvantages include the fact that rayon frequently is not washable, tends to lose strength when wet and lacks the easy-care qualities of all-synthetic fibers.

One modification in rayon fibers in recent years has added greater strength, especially when the fabric is wet, thus giving it a greater dimensional stability in washing. This modified form is known as "high wet modulus rayon." The original type, still the most widely produced, is known as viscose rayon. Another major type, cuprammonium rayon, is usually produced in finer filaments and yarns which are used in lightweight sheer and semi-sheer fabrics and also is sometimes combined with cotton to make fabrics with uneven textured surfaces.

The rayon filament can be highly twisted, making it desirable for crepe fabrics, which have a pebbly surface created by the twists in the fiber. Rayon can imitate linen or be combined with linen to increase wrinkle resistance and pleat retention. It can also be a low-cost substitute for more expensive fabrics where a silky look is required. Rayon can be processed or finished to have many different textures and hands.

## Sewing with Rayons

Rayon materials are not difficult to manage in home sewing. For lightweight fabrics, use size 11 needle, nylon thread, moderate tension (test on scraps) and soft styling. For the heavier, two-ply rayons that often resemble linen, use a size 14 needle and mercerized thread.

## The Care of Rayon Clothes

Following the fabric manufacturer's instructions is important in the care of rayons, especially when the fabric contains other fibers as well. Generally the following procedures will be safe:

If the rayon fabric is washable, wash by hand using lukewarm water and suds, gently squeezing them through the garments. Be sure to rinse thoroughly because undissolved suds may dull colored garments and make whites look cloudy. Don't wring the garment. Smooth out on a nonrust hanger. Iron while damp on the reverse side with a medium-hot iron (about 300°F., or at the rayon setting). If the right side needs a touch-up, use a press cloth.

If you have any doubts whether the fabric is washable, have it drycleaned.

## Rayon Trademarks

There are more than fifty rayon trademarks assigned to the major fiber producers. While trademarks are always useful to know because the larger manufacturers protect them with follow-through quality control, the rayon trademarks are less known to the consumer than those for the highly promoted synthetics. And unless you are aware of the specific properties of each trademarked rayon, the trademark may have little meaning. More important in selection of the fabric are identification of its contents and the care instructions. Some of the major rayon trademarks for apparel are:

*Avril*: FMC Corporation (American Viscose Division).
*Bemberg*: Beaunit Corporation.

*Coloray*: Courtauld's North American Inc.
*Enkrome*: American Enka Company.
*Nupron*: IRC Fibers Company (American Cyanamid Company).
*Zantrel*: American Enka Company.


# The Acetates

Acetate was introduced commercially in the United States by the Celanese Corporation in 1924.

The fiber is made by combining cellulose with acetate from acetic acid and acetic anhydride. This is dissolved in acetone for extrusion through the spinneret and, as the filaments emerge, warm air evaporates the solvent leaving a fiber of cellulose acetate.

Note that acetone is used in the dissolving process. Acetone is also capable of dissolving part of your acetate dress if spilled on it. Some nail polish removers and perfumes contain this type of solvent, so be careful.

The most common apparel use of acetate is in dressy fabrics. This is largely due to its high luster, which is essential in such cloths as satin, taffeta and other formal fabrics. Also, acetate's heat sensitivity makes it possible to emboss or moiré the cloth.

I have a personal tender spot for acetate. My first meeting with it was in the early 1930s when the Celanese Corporation in Canada was searching for some unknown talent to design an evening gown in its new satins and moirés for promotional purposes. In those days, it was de rigeur for a high school girl to own a formal dress, and since, like just about everyone I knew, I could sew, I entered the competition. It still gives me moments of pleasant nostalgia to remember my creation, which was selected, commercially reproduced and exhibited in the largest store in Montreal.

Today the acetates have been much improved, but they are still available in all the old patterns, as well as in newer surrahs and silklike surfaces. Some of the modern acetate fabrics are beautifully printed, approximating the look of printed silks at considerably lower cost. One of the main features of acetate, in fact, is its ability to take a wide range of colors. Other favorable properties include excellent draping qualities, good dimensional stability and a luxurious feel and appearance.

One of the major uses for acetate is in linings, because of its low cost.

## Sewing Tips for Acetates

Sew acetates the way you would silk—using a fine needle, silk or nylon thread, and moderate tension. Handle the fabric gently, and use a low to medium setting on the iron when pressing.

## Tips on Care of Acetates

Most acetate fabrics must be dry cleaned. If washable, hand-wash in warm suds without rubbing, rinse thoroughly and gently press the water out without twisting. Hang on a rustproof hanger to dry. Iron while damp on the wrong side at moderate heat. If finishing touches are needed on the right side, use a press cloth.

# Trademarks

Major acetate trademarks and trade names include:

*Acele*: E. I. du Pont de Nemours and Company, Inc.
*Avisco*: FMC Corporation (American Viscose Division).
*Celanese Acetate*: Celanese Corporation.
*Celaperm*: Celanese Corporation.
*Chromspun*: Eastman Kodak Company.
*Estron*: Eastman Kodak Company.

# The Triacetates

Triacetate is related to acetate and the production is somewhat similar except that the proportion of acetate to cellulose is higher.

In properties, however, there are important differences. Most significant is triacetate's ability to withstand heat, which makes it possible to set permanent pleats, machine-wash the fabric and use higher temperatures in pressing. Triacetate requires much less ironing, if any, than acetate fabrics.

Triacetate can be given a crisp finish, as in sharkskin and other woven cloths. It can also have good drapeability, as in tricots and single-knit jersey.

There is only one trademark for triacetate—"Arnel," which is used by Celanese Corporation in promotion of approved fabrics containing its triacetate filament and staple products.

In sewing woven triacetates, follow the same guidelines as for acetate, but use nylon or polyester thread. For triacetate knits, you can use the same instructions given for polyester knits.

As for care, check the labels carefully. Pleated garments will retain their shape better if hand-washed. All other triacetates can be machine-washed and tumble-dried unless the manufacturer says otherwise.

## Some Wholesale Resources

Following is a list of wholesale resources specializing in rayons, acetates and triacetates which sell to retail fabric shops:

*Award Fabrics, 1412 Broadway, New York City:* Printed knits in acetates and blends, some quilted.

*Belding Corticelli, 1430 Broadway, New York City:* Novelties in knits and woven fabrics, with matched notions. Wide variety.

*Bloomsberg Inc., 525 Seventh Avenue, New York City:* Dressy fabrics, crepes, satins.

*Blue Ridge-Winkler, 119 West 40th Street, New York City:* Knit goods, strong in the "Arnel" knits, double-knits and tricot, prints and plain.

*Charter Fabrics, Inc., 1001 Avenue of the Americas, New York City:* Tailored rayons, print and plain, also acetates in seersuckers and checks.

*Cohama Fabrics, Inc., 1407 Broadway, New York City:* Wide variety of tailored and dressy fabrics.

*Folker Fabrics Corporation, 1071 Avenue of the Americas, New York City:* Large group of Arnel fabrics, woven as well as warp knits.

*Harold Friend, Inc., 251 West 39th Street, New York City:* Taffetas, both plain and quilted.

*Gallery, 1412 Broadway, New York City:* Outstanding print house for acetates and other fabrics. Unusual designs.

*Loomskill, Inc., 1412 Broadway, New York City:* Interesting prints in rayons, acetates and other fabrics.

*Pemly Fabrics, 1001 Avenue of the Americas, New York City:* Rayon brocades, dressy fabrics.

*Shirley Fabrics Corporation, 1412 Broadway, New York City:* Rayon-linen type, other tailored cloths.

# X

# Nylon–The First All-Synthetic Fiber

THE BIRTH OF nylon was announced by DuPont in 1938.

I met this first "miracle fiber" in 1939 at the New York World's Fair in the form of beautiful sheer stockings. Until then most hosiery was made of silk, which was lovely in texture and cling, but more opaque. Women who flocked to the DuPont exhibit had never realized how transparent everyday hose could be, a transparency made possible by the great strength of the fine threads that can be produced from nylon fibers. Until then, silk had been the strongest fiber used in any type of apparel. The idea that fabrics made completely from chemicals would revolutionize the clothes we wore seemed like science fiction then.

Nylon went on to great things. Shortly after the first stockings came on the market, nylon was off to war in parachutes and other military products (while nylon stockings became trading items on the black market).

93

After World War II, nylon fibers, in a variety of modifications, went back into improved hosiery, into easily washable and quick-drying lingerie, into automobile tires, into carpets and upholstery and many industrial products.

In dress fabrics, nylon's outstanding use has been in lightweight knits, popularized by easy-to-pack, crush-resistant travel dresses. The 100 percent woven nylons have been used mainly in lingerie, linings and wind- and rain-resistant sportswear.

More recently DuPont has introduced a new trademarked variety called "Qiana," which may broaden the uses of nylon in apparel considerably. It has greater versatility for women's dress use than any previous nylon and can be made up into either knit or woven fabrics, with the closest approach to the luxurious feel of silk yet achieved by any man-made fiber. At the same time, "Qiana" fabrics may be easily machine-washed or dry cleaned, are wrinkle resistant, and have good shape retention, durability and color fastness.

## The Properties of Nylon

Nylon fibers are produced like other synthetics by the process of extruding a syrupy mixture of chemical compounds (for nylon, polyamides) through a spinneret, then cooling and stretching the filaments to produce the desired properties for each intended use. The filaments are then processed into either filament yarn or staple yarn, depending on end use.

There are now more than twenty companies in the United States producing nylon fibers or yarns for varied consumer and industrial products. Each of the many types of fiber and/or yarn is specially "engineered" for the product into which it will go, but all members of the nylon family have similar basic characteristics. These include:

- greater strength and resistance to abrasion than any other fiber—nylon's most important properties;
- low moisture absorbency, which makes nylon fabrics easy to wash and dry (but sometimes not too comfortable to wear);
- good recovery from stretching and crushing;
- light weight, enhancing its value for outerwear such as windbreaker jackets as well as for knit dresses;
- an ability to take dyes in a range of colors.

Many modifications over the years, made either chemically or mechanically, have improved nylon's desirable apparel properties and reduced or overcome some of its less desirable qualities. The most significant changes were accomplished by texturizing, a process that is important in all synthetic textiles and is described in Chapter III. Texturized nylons have a softer feel and better wrinkle resistance, are more opaque (less "see-through") in lighter-weight fabrics and have better stretch recovery.

Also important in nylon apparel fabrics are the variations that have been developed by adding chemicals to the fiber-making compounds. These additives become part of the fiber itself. Their use has enabled nylon producers to make the fabric more moisture-absorbing, which increases its comfort in wear and reduces the static electricity that causes clinging; to improve its resistance to heat, light, yellowing and soiling; and, where required, to make the fabric duller and less transparent, (which is important in sheer clothes).

In selecting a nylon fabric, your main guidelines will

be the kind of garment you want to make, the feel and look of the cloth, the manufacturer's care instructions and a quality trademark which is backed up by a major fiber producer.

# Trademarks

Some of the major trademark names used in nylon fabrics sold at retail are:

*Antron* (DuPont): Yarns produce a lustrous fabric with good color that will tailor well into soft dresses, blouses and at-home wear.

*Blue "C" Nylon* (Monsanto): Trademark for varied types of Monsanto nylon fibers and yarns.

*Caprolan* (Allied Chemical): Varied filament yarns.

*Celanese Nylon* (Celanese Corporation): Various types of yarns for both knit and woven nylon fabrics.

*DuPont Nylon* (DuPont): Trademark for basic fibers used in a number of nylon fabrics.

*Enkalure* (American Enka): Trademark for an untexturized yarn that makes up into smooth, flowing dressy fabrics.

*Qiana* (DuPont): A new nylon being heavily promoted; fabrics must meet rigid performance and marketing standards. Fabrics have silklike feel and appearance.

Nylon is occasionally blended with other fibers, primarily to lend its strength to the finished fabric or for decorative purposes.

## Sewing with Nylon

The general instructions for sewing with nylon, including "Qiana," are similar to those for other all-synthetics.

Use only nylon or polyester thread. For woven fabrics, use a size 11 needle and 10 to 12 stitches per inch. For knits, use a ballpoint needle and 12 to 15 stitches per inch. Maintain a moderate, balanced tension on the sewing machine and guide the fabric, both in back and in front of the needle, with a light but firm hold to avoid puckering.

"Qiana" requires higher pressing temperatures (low wool setting with steam) than other nylons. On all nylons other than "Qiana," steam-press at prescribed setting indicated on your iron, or about 275° F., on reverse side of the fabric. If steam iron is not available, use a damp press cloth. Press seams closed first, then open. Allow fabric to cool before removing from ironing board. Paper inserts may be used under seam allowances to avoid marking the fabric's surface.

It is advisable to test both the machine stitch and iron heat in advance on scraps of material.

In washable clothes, all components (linings, trim, etc.) must also be washable and shrinkproof.

All knits should be relaxed overnight by spreading the fabric flat on a table. Don't let any part of the fabric hang over the edge.

## Taking Care of Nylon Clothes

The most important single recommendation that can be given about the care of nylon—or clothes made of any synthetic—is: Follow the instructions of the fabric manufacturer *closely*. As noted, nylon fibers are produced in many variations. Your fabric may be a blend of nylon and some other fiber, and fabric finishes vary.

Having said this, there are some general rules on which most textile people agree, and these are given here merely as guidelines. If you follow them, the chances are that you will be safe.

When washing, machine drying or ironing fabric that contains other fibers besides nylon, always use the temperatures suggested for the most heat-sensitive fiber.

Nylon garments, both knits and wovens, can be hand- or machine-washed. (This assumes that you have used nonshrink linings, bindings, decoration, trim, etc. If not, have dry cleaned.)

Before washing, pretreat heavily soiled areas by rubbing them with a paste of detergent and water. Grease and oil stains should be removed *before washing* with a dry cleaning fluid or dry spot remover.

In machine washing, use warm water and detergent. If no dryer is available, remove the garment wet after its rinse cycle—before the final spin-drying cycle—and drip-dry. If you have a home dryer with a low heat setting, let the washer go through its whole spin-dry cycle, then put the garment in the dryer at low or medium heat. Remove *immediately* after the dryer stops.

Hand-wash in warm (not hot) water with detergent suds. Don't twist or wring the garment, but gently squeeze the suds through. A cold-water detergent such as those developed for washable wools may also be used. Rinse thoroughly in lukewarm water until all suds are removed. A fabric softener may be added to the final rinse water, especially in hard-water areas. This will help reduce static. Gently squeeze out as much of the water as possible and drip-dry.

White and pastel nylons must be washed separately from the darker colors because of nylon's tendency to absorb color, and thoroughly rinsed to avoid graying. Whites should be bleached with a chlorine bleach or optical whitening agent. Follow the manufacturer's instructions carefully when bleaching. If none are given, use those for cotton.

Nylon knits should require no ironing. Woven fabrics can be lightly pressed or touched up with an iron at the "rayon" or synthetic setting. Safe temperatures are between 275° and 300°F., depending on the type of nylon. "Qiana," however, should be steam-pressed at the low wool setting.

## Some Wholesale Resources

Among textile companies that sell nylons directly to retail fabric stores are:

*Amer-Mill, 119 West 40th Street, New York City:* "Qiana" nylons.

*Armo Company, 206 West 40th Street, New York City:* Knitted nylons for lingerie, bathing suits.

*Blue Ridge Winkler, 119 West 40th Street, New York City:* Knitted nylons for dress wear.

*Burlington Retail (Burlington Industries), 1345 Avenue of the Americas, New York City:* A large selection of nylons, nylon blends and "Qiana."

*Carletex Fabrics, 1451 Broadway, New York City:* Antron nylons, warp knits.

*Couleur International, Ltd., 1412 Broadway, New York City:* "Qiana" prints.

*Folker Fabrics Corporation, 1071 Avenue of the Americas, New York City:* A good selection of nylon knits.

*Foxco Fabrics, 1412 Broadway, New York City:* All types of nylon knits, including warp knits.

*French Fabrics, 180 Madison Avenue, New York City:* Warp and other nylon knits.

# XI
## Polyester–The Fiber That Made Wash-and-Wear a Reality

THE POLYESTER FAMILY of fibers—formed from chemical elements derived from petroleum, coal, air and water—has in less than a generation become number-one among synthetics in apparel use. It has created whole new concepts in clothing (wash-and-wear, durable press, crushproof travel knits), and in the process it has competitively spurred some remarkable improvements in all types of products, including cottons and wools.

The properties that polyester fibers lend to textiles include outstanding wrinkle resistance and resiliency; wash-and-wear qualities and ability to blend with other fibers; excellent dimensional stability in cleaning and wearing; strength and resistance to abrasion; good resistance to perspiration, chemicals and mildew; and an exceptional ability to retain pressed-in pleats when these are set by heat.

The enormous popularity of polyester, especially in

blends and streetwear knits, has demonstrated that these properties far outweigh its deficiencies, one of which is its harsh hand, which is most noticeable in the woven fabrics. In blends, the softness of cotton compensates for this to some extent, and new texturizing processes applied to both the horizontal filling threads and the vertical warp threads should also improve polyester in this respect. Another disadvantage is that oil and grease stains tend to cling tenaciously to polyester. This is overcome in part by new soil-release finishes. New types of polyesters now being developed are expected to overcome these and other drawbacks to polyester. One of these, developed by Monsanto and trademarked "Spectran," claims to do just that.

Polyester was developed in England in 1941 and was produced commercially about nine years later simultaneously by DuPont (trademark, "Dacron") in the United States and Imperial Chemical Industries (trademark, "Terrylene") in England. With expiration of the patent rights in 1958, a number of other major chemical companies entered the field, and a huge jump in production followed. In 1950, the United States used about 25 million pounds of polyester fibers (including imports). By 1970, the figure had soared to approximately 1.5 *billion* pounds—sixty times as much. The beginning of polyester's greatest growth coincided with the introduction of durable press in 1961.

## Polyester Blends

The popularity of polyester in apparel is due not only to its special properties but also to its versatility in adapting to various weaves and knits without losing any of these properties. It blends with other fibers, both natural and synthetic, without destroying their desirable features and often eliminates some of their faults.

When used in woven fabrics, polyester most frequently is blended with other fibers. If the consumer wants the performance of polyester, there must be at least 50 percent polyester in the heavier blends such as wool and at least 65 percent in the lighter weights such as single-ply cottons and rayons. In the very lightweight fabrics—such as georgettes and chiffons—100 percent polyester produces highly attractive fabrics with all the special properties of polyester.

In the knits, polyester is often used unblended, for its yarns can be knitted into a large number of designs and weights. Polyester knits, in my opinion, form the all-time great travel wardrobe—especially the double-knits. Polyester also combines successfully with wool yarns for winter wear and with other knit yarns for high-fashion effect.

## Sewing with Polyesters

Some suggestions for sewing with polyester or polyester blend fabrics:

First, all the notions that the garment will require should be polyester or nylon—thread, zipper, binding and any other trim.

The zipper should be preshrunk by placing it for a few minutes in hot water, drying and pressing the tape. (Do not press the zipper teeth.)

For woven polyesters and blends, use a number 11 needle for lightweight fabrics and a number 14 needle for heavier materials. For knits, use a ballpoint needle.

Top and bobbin tension on the sewing machine must be balanced. Synthetic fabrics require a lower tension than natural cloths. Test out the tension on a few scraps until you are satisfied with it.

For knits, a number of fiber producers recommend washing the fabric to preshrink it before cutting. I also like to leave any knitted fabric overnight on a table, spread loosely and not overhanging an edge. This will relax the fabric and ensure much better fit for the life of the garment.

## The Basics of Polyester Care

The care of polyester and polyester blends has been simplified by modern washing machines, dryers and irons that have precise heat settings for the various fabrics. Whether or not you have the latest type of household equipment, there are some simple rules to follow:

Clothes in which all trimmings are compatible with the basic fabric of the garment can be machine-washed and tumble-dried. But they must be washed in warm, not hot, water, machine-dried at *low* heat and ironed with a warm, not hot, iron. Be sure to spot-clean all oil and grease stains *before washing*—in fact, as soon as they occur. Try soaking the spot in detergent and warm water or use a cleaning fluid. If you are uncertain about the trimmings, polyester fabrics can also be dry cleaned.

These general instructions would be superseded, of course, by any care instructions that come with the fabric. And they apply only when the *major* constituent of the fabric is polyester. If there is more rayon than polyester in the fabric, for example, you must treat it like a rayon.

The major trademarked names for polyester include:

*Avlin:* American Viscose Division, FMC Corporation.
*Blue "C" Polyester:* Monsanto Company.
*Dacron:* E. I. du Pont de Nemours and Company.
*Encron:* American Enka Company.
*Fortrel:* Fiber Industries (Celanese Corporation).
*Kodel:* Eastman Chemical Products, Inc.
*Spectran:* Monsanto Company.
*Trevira:* Hoechst Fibers Inc.
*Vycron:* Beaunit Corporation.

## Wholesale Resources

The following mills, converters and wholesalers are among those that sell polyester fabrics to retail stores:

*Abbot Fabrics, 1412 Broadway, New York City:* Printed and plain, woven and knitted fabrics.

*Ameritex, 1412 Broadway, New York City:* Polyesters and blends.

*Bloomberg, Inc., 525 Seventh Avenue, New York City:* Woven texturized polyesters.

*Burlington Retail (Burlington Industries), 1345 Avenue of the Americas, New York City:* This includes Klopman Fabrics. Large selection of interesting blends.

*Chelsea Textiles, 1071 Avenue of the Americas, New York City:* Large selection of polyester knits.

*Cohama Fabrics, Inc., 1407 Broadway, New York City:* Wide variety of polyester knits, wovens, prints.

*Fabrics by Berlin Woolen Company, 247 West 38th Street, New York City:* All types of polyester knits and wovens.

*Gold Mills, 1430 Broadway, New York City:* All types of knits, novelty and plain wovens.

*Hayden Retail Corporation, 1412 Broadway, New York City:* Polyester double-knits and warp knits, prints and plain.

*William Heller, 1071 Avenue of the Americas, New York City:* A leading knit firm; all types of high-quality polyester knits.

*Inwood Knitting Mills, 119 West 40th Street, New York City:* Polyester knits (also acrylic, cotton and blend knits).

*Lawson Fabrics, Inc., 1001 Avenue of the Americas, New York City:* Double-knit and jacquard polyesters.

*Quorum Fabrics, 108 West 39th Street, New York City:* Interesting double-knits, novelties; well-styled fabrics.

*Stehli Fabrics, 119 West 40th Street, New York City:* Fine-quality double-knits.

*J. P. Stevens, 1185 Avenue of the Americas, New York City:* One of the largest collections of fabrics for retail selling. All fibers, wovens and knits.

*Steps in the manufacture of fabric and samples of wools and various synthetic weaves, illustrating the variety of colors and textures available today.*

1. A close-up view of one form of man-made fiber spinning—the melt-extrusion of polymer through small holes.

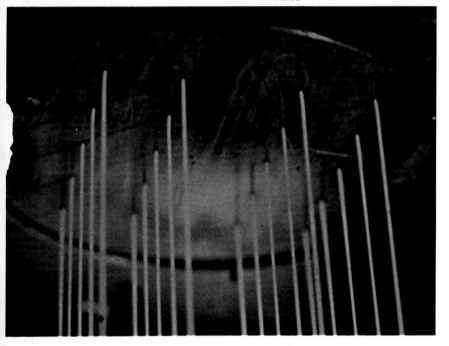

2. Spinneret.
HOECHST

3. Fibers are spun on
high-powered machines.
HOECHST

4. Thousands of pounds of fibers are created every day.
HOECHST

5 & 6. Quality
testing and
control are vital
aspects of the
fabric industry.
HOECHST

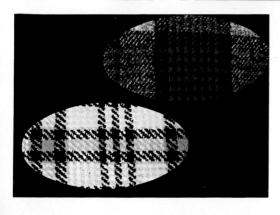

7. 100% wool plaids.
WOOL BUREAU

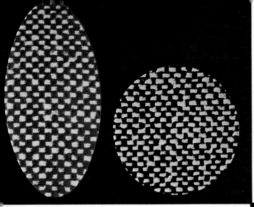

8. 100% wool tweeds.

WOOL BUREAU

9. 100% wool knits and
woven fabric in
coordinated colors.

WOOL BUREAU

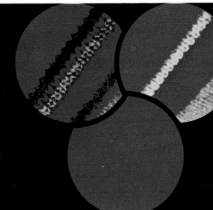

10. Three different crepe weaves.

WOOL BUREAU

11. 70% textured acetate/30%
fortrel polyester
warp knits by Celanese.

CELANESE

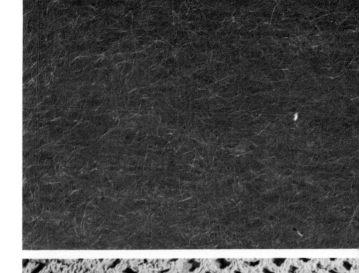

12. Mohair
swatches
MOHAIR COUNCIL

13. Arnel/nylon
raschel knit.
CELANESE

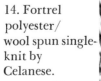

14. Fortrel
polyester/
wool spun single-
knit by
Celanese.
CELANESE

15. 100% fortrel
polyester double-knit.

**CELANESE**

16. Arnel triacetate/nylon
warp knit by Celanese.

**CELANESE**

17. Single-knit jerseys
of "Qiana," Antron
and blends by Du Pont.

**DU PONT**

18. Knits of polyester and nylon,
dacron and cotton by Du Pont.

19. Brushed surface fabrics by Du Pont.

20. Dacron and wool blends by Du Pont.

21. Trevira knits by Hoechst Fibers.

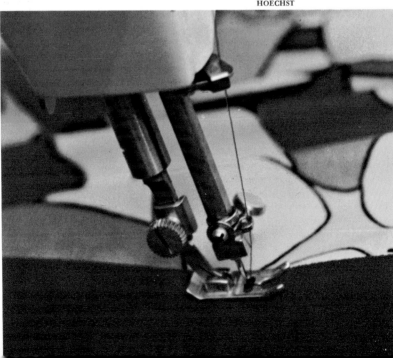

# ⚜XII
# *Acrylics–Synthetic Rival of Wool*

THE NAMES NYLON, rayon and polyester are easily identifiable, but many women might find it difficult to identify *acrylic* immediately, for though the acrylics constitute an important family of synthetics, they are most readily recognizable under their trademarked names ("Orlon," "Acrilan," "Creslan," "Zefran," etc.), which have been widely advertised and promoted.

Acrylics are the synthetic substitutes for wool. They are very popular in sweaters, knit and woven fabrics, carpeting, blankets, knitting yarns and pile and fleece fabrics. Their main importance to people who sew is that they can provide an adequate replacement for many wools at substantially lower cost. Some of the newer acrylic fabrics approach the quality of the finest wools. In addition, acrylic fabrics are easier to care for than wool and provide excellent warmth with very light weight.

In comparing acrylics and wools, it should be noted

that you will not be able to find acrylic fabrics in many forms that are available in wools. Because the fiber is light and soft, it will not make up into yarns comparable to those used in wool worsteds such as serge, gabardine, covert cloth and similar hard-finished cloths.

## Production and Special Properties

Acrylic fibers were first developed and commercially produced in the United States by DuPont in 1950, followed in the next several years by Monsanto, Dow Badische and American Cyanamid.

The basic acrylic fiber differs considerably from both nylon and polyester although it is chemically constructed. The fiber is produced from acrylonitrile—a colorless liquid derived from elements in coal, air, water, petroleum and limestone. Small amounts of other chemicals are added to improve its dyeability and various modifications are made for different end uses. Like the other synthetics, the fiber is formed as a filament by extrusion through a spinneret. However, it is mainly used in staple form (which makes it possible to bulk the yarn) and is crimped during the fiber-making process before being cut into staple length.

The qualities that distinguish the acrylics are, first and foremost, their resemblance to wool in hand and appearance, their warmth and very light weight, colorfastness, good dimensional stability and resiliency, and resistance to moths, sunlight, oil and chemicals—plus wash-and-wear qualities the wools do not possess.

Because acrylic fabrics can be made in very light weights, they can be set in permanent sunburst pleats —even the double-knit fabrics. In the lighter weights, both woven and knitted acrylics are often used in this manner.

There are many variations of acrylic fiber, producing equally varied fabrics. Acrylic yarns are most often bulked to give a soft, fluffy construction to the fabric. Some acrylics are woven into such fine and light cloths as challis. A new DuPont variety, merchandised under the name "Nomelle," has a soft luxurious hand approaching that of cashmere wool and is featherweight light.

Knit acrylic fabrics come in circular single- and double-knits as well as in warp and raschel novelty knits. The raschel knits are particularly popular because the bright colors that acrylics will take, combined with the versatility of the raschel machines, have produced a host of interesting designs.

Note should also be made of the popularity of acrylic yarns for home knitting. In 1970, 4 percent of all acrylic fibers produced in the United States went into yarn for home knitting, and this percentage may have increased substantially since.

The use of acrylics in pile and fleece fabrics will be dealt with in the following chapter.

## Acrylic Trademarks

Among the best-known trademarks for acrylic are:

*Acrilan*: Monsanto Company.
*Creslan*: American Cyanamid Company.
*Orlon:* E. I. du Pont de Nemours and Company, Inc.
*Zefkrome*: Dow Badische Company.
*Zefran*: Dow Badische Company.

# Care of Acrylic Clothes

As with all synthetic fabrics, follow the manufacturer's care instructions. Acrylic fabrics may be washed or dry cleaned, depending on the nature of the particular fabric and the type of soiling. For a garment to be washable, every part of it must be able to undergo washing. Blended fabric must be handled with the care required for the most sensitive fiber in the blend. If washing is in order, the following methods recommended by the Man-Made Fiber Producers Association will generally be safe for acrylics.

Wash delicate items by hand in warm water with soap or detergent. Rinse thoroughly in warm water and use a fabric softener in the rinse water. Gently squeeze out water, smooth or shake out garment and let dry on a nonrust hanger. (Sweaters should be dried flat.)

When machine washing, use warm water and a fabric softener during the final rinse cycle. Machine-dry at *low* temperature setting. Remove garments from dryer as soon as tumbling cycle is complete.

If ironing is required, use a moderately warm (never hot) iron. A safe ironing temperature is 300° to 325°F.

# Sewing with Acrylics

In sewing woven acrylic fabrics, the same instructions should be followed as for polyesters. (See page 103.) For acrylic knits, use the same guidelines as for nylon knits. (See page 97.) The thread should be nylon.

## Some Wholesale Resources

Among textile mills and converters who sell acrylic fabrics to retail shops are:

*Award Fabrics, 1412 Broadway, New York City*: Acrylic prints.

*Beaunit Counter Fabrics, 261 Madison Avenue, New York City*: Large selection of synthetic knits, including acrylics.

*Blends-Mag-Knit, 1001 Avenue of the Americas, New York City*: Acrylic knits, including sweater-stitch types.

*Concord Fabrics, 1411 Broadway, New York City*: Acrylic knits and wovens.

*Deering Milliken, Inc., 1045 Avenue of the Americas, New York City*: Large producer of woven and knit acrylics, many patterns.

*Inwood Knitting Mills, 119 West 40th Street, New York City*: Acrylic knits.

*Logantex, Inc., 1450 Broadway, New York City*: Synthetic plaids.

# ✠XIII
## *Fake Furs, Deep-Pile and Fleece Fabrics*

FOR EXPERIENCED SEWERS the fake furs, deep-pile and fleece fabrics—used in clothing largely for outerwear—offer an opportunity to try something new. Some fabric shops carry a good selection.

## Modacrylics

The synthetic furs are made mainly of modacrylic (modified acrylic) and acrylic fibers. Modacrylic fabrics in particular can closely imitate real fur by having both long top fibers and short, dense fibers under them, thus simulating the guard hair and undercoat of fur. This is possible because modacrylic fibers can be produced with controlled shrinkages. When fibers with different shrinkage properties are knitted or woven into pile fabrics, passing the fabric through heat results in a furlike surface as the fibers shrink to different lengths.

Because modacrylics soften at low temperatures they can be stretched, embossed or molded into many surface patterns.

The ingenuity of the fiber producers and textile manufacturers has produced synthetic furs that imitate seal, leopard, mink, fox, Persian lamb and a host of other animal furs. The popularity of these fabrics is due to their inexpensiveness, lightness and warmth—and also to the fact that many women these days don't want to wear animal skins.

Modacrylic fibers are produced from combinations of acrylonitrile (the base for acrylics) and other chemicals. The compounds are mixed with solvents that reduce them to a gelatinous consistency. As with the other synthetics, this mixture is forced through holes in a spinneret to produce the fiber filaments. The solvents are removed by drying in warm air (dry spinning) and the fibers are gathered into long bundles of tow, which is crimped to give them the texture and bulk required for most end uses, then cut into staple length for spinning into yarn.

Modacrylic fibers were first produced commercially in the United States in 1949 by Union Carbide Corporation (trademark, "Dynel"). Other producers are Eastman Kodak ("Verel") and Monsanto ("Elura" and "SEF").

In addition to their use in synthetic furs and other deep-pile fabrics, modacrylics are probably best known to women in the form of wigs. They also are found in carpets (in combination with acrylics) and in draperies and curtains because of their unusual fire-retardant qualities. It is claimed that a new modacrylic, "SEF," recently introduced by Monsanto, has superior flame retardation, plus good drapeability and dyeability.

"SEF" is aimed primarily at the children's sleepwear market.

The deep-pile fabrics, mainly acrylics and modacrylics, have been very successful in coats and jackets, which can be made at home by the more knowledgeable sewer.

Pile fabrics with shorter naps lend themselves to interesting designs for at-home loungewear. They also can be used to make a warm lining for coats of lightweight material, such as rainwear.

For napped goods other than those with a furry or deep-pile look, there is a wide variety of natural and synthetic fabrics, including cottons in corduroys and velveteens, silk, rayon and polyester velvets, and many woolens and synthetics with brushed surfaces. Among the newer synthetic pile fabrics are colorful brushed plaids.

## Sewing with Fake Fur and Pile Fabrics

Pile fabrics require special handling in home sewing. The following instructions are suggested for the experienced—and patient—woman.

- All napped goods should be cut in one direction. Be sure to decide in advance which way you want the nap to go.
- Avoid all unnecessary seams.
- Fold back the cloth for facings instead of cutting them separately.
- Use polyester staple thread.
- Closings should take loops or hooks, rather than regular buttonholes. If you must have buttonholes, bind them off with leather or preshrunk ribbon.

- The pattern should be cut singly and not on the fold. Outline one side with chalk, then reverse the pattern and outline the other side.
- For cutting, use a sharp single-edged razor blade, as you would for fur.
- When using a zigzag stitch, cut away the pile in the seam allowance *before* stitching. With a straight stitch, cut away the pile in the seam allowance *after* stitching. Press open the seam allowances with fingers only. Never use an iron or steam.
- Machine tension should be balanced and light. Use a size 14 needle and 8 to 10 stitches per inch.
- Instead of basting, pin the garment up with colored pins.
- On shoulder and neckline seams, stitch on a narrow preshrunk tape to prevent stretching.

## Care of Fake Fur and Other Pile Fabrics

*All* deep-pile garments, regardless of fiber content, should be dry cleaned or fur cleaned, depending on the fabric.

As for other types of napped goods, some may be washable, but it is essential to follow the manufacturer's care instructions. Washability will depend on many factors, including the specific type of fiber or fibers and the depth of the pile.

## Wholesale Resources

Among textile firms supplying synthetic fur, deep-pile and other napped fabrics to retail yard good stores are:

*Borg Textiles Division, (Bunker-Ramo Corporation), 104 West 40th Street, New York City*: All types of synthetic fake furs and pile fabrics.

*Collins and Airkman, 210 Madison Avenue, New York City*: Furlike fabrics, particularly "seal"; also plaids and fancies suitable for loungewear, linings, etc.

*Glenoit Mills, Inc., 114 West 40th Street, New York City*: Fake furs, pile fabrics, plaids, stripes, all in deep pile suitable for apparel or articles for the home.

*Malden Mills, 450 Seventh Avenue, New York City*: Animal prints and plain-pile fabrics for outerwear and decorative use.

*Norwood Mills, 49 West 37th Street, New York City*: Imitation animal skins, heavy pile.

# XIV
# S-T-R-E-T-C-H Fabrics

THE NEWEST GENERATION of apparel textiles are fabrics that give with the body, don't bind or tug and allow full freedom of movement along with a sleek, figure-controlling shape. These are the stretch fabrics.

Stretchability, which made double-knits so popular in the 1960s, is now being built into many other types of fabrics that previously had a more rigid construction, including wovens in virtually all fibers and weights.

Just a few years back, stretch fabrics were used almost exclusively in girdles, bras, bathing suits, support hose and ski pants. Today they are used to make up coats, suits, dresses, skirts, sweaters, body shirts, underwear and other apparel. Stretch fabrics can be found in most yard goods shops or departments and the variety of materials available should increase rapidly in the next few years. In the textile industry, I found great enthusiasm for these new stretch fabrics and an almost unanimous opinion that they would soon account for a big proportion of all apparel textiles. The main reason is that these fabrics—which recover swiftly from stretching or crushing—can be made of practically any fiber or mixture of fibers, natural or synthetic, and have the look, feel and other properties of the fiber or blend used.

## How They Get Their Stretch

The newer stretch materials owe their existence to two important scientific-engineering achievements.

One was the development of synthetic elastic fibers, which have displaced rubber in apparel textiles. The first of these was spandex, introduced in 1959, a remarkable man-made fiber (consisting mainly of polyurethane) which has greater elasticity than rubber and is far superior to rubber in resistance to damage by body oils and cosmetic lotions, sunlight, flexing or bending and abrasion. Current forms of spandex can be stretched up to six or seven times their relaxed length and will snap back immediately. In 1970, a new elastic fiber, anidex, was introduced commercially. Anidex (made from monohydric alcohol and acrylic acid) does not have the stretch and holding power of spandex, but it can take higher temperatures in washing, drying and ironing and is said to have superior resistance to chemicals.

The second factor spurring the growth of stretch fabrics was the invention of core-spinning. In this method of making yarn, staple-length fibers—either natural or synthetic—are spun around a tiny core of spandex or anidex fiber. The outer fibers give the yarn its appearance and properties, to which spandex or anidex add stretch and fast recovery. Thus we get stretchable cottons, polyesters, rayons, acrylics, worsteds and various combinations. Core-spun yarns and fabrics are produced in many different weights, from a fine batiste to an outerwear worsted. The fabrics may have either one-way or two-way stretch, depending on whether core-spun yarn is used in both directions in the fabric or in only one.

Anidex fibers also can be blended in very small quantities (5 to 10 percent) with cotton, wool, linen or staple-length synthetic fibers to produce a cloth that has the look and all the characteristics of the main fiber—plus elasticity.

Core-spun fabrics are generally more expensive than their conventional sisters, or than other types of stretch fabrics. You will know a fabric is core-spun if the identifying tag or label indicates that it contains one of the spandex fibers. Among the better-known trademarked names for spandex are "Lycra" (DuPont), "Numa" (Ameliotex), "Glospan" (Globe Manufacturing Company) and "Unel" (Union Carbide). Anidex was developed and is produced by Rohm and Haas Company, under the trademarked name "Anim/8."

There are two other principal methods of putting stretch into fabrics.

One is the heat-stretch method, used with nylons and polyesters. This process involves twisting or coiling the synthetic filament yarn tightly, then setting the twist with heat. When made into fabric, these yarns thus have built-in springs which uncoil and stretch when pulled, then go back into shape. This process gives long-lasting stretch performance; the fabrics can be manufactured with either horizontal or vertical stretch, or both. If the fabric is stated to contain "stretch nylon" or "stretch polyester" it will most often be made of heat-set yarn.

Another process, mechanical-chemical stretch, is applied to the fabric itself, not the yarn. This involves the use of chemicals and tension or heat. The fabrics do not have as much stretch as those produced by core-spun or heat-stretch methods, recovery is usually slow and the give is usually only one way—horizontally. Mechanical stretch is used mainly in cottons, cotton blends, wools and rayons, and only in wovens, not knits.

## What to Look for in Stretch Fabrics

When shopping for stretch fabrics it would be wise to know in advance not only the kind of garment you want to make, but also the direction in which you want the stretch and the amount of stretch you will need. For example, a worsted that stretches in width may be equally useful in a jacket—where the pull is across the shoulders and upper arms—and in pants—where horizontal stretch may be desirable in the seat. However, if you are planning to make ski pants with stirrups, you will want either vertical or two-way stretch, and a greater degree of stretch. (For clothes for all active sports, two-way stretch is recommended.) Also, while stretch fabrics may be ideal for form-fitting dresses, because they provide a clingier look with far greater comfort, they are hardly needed in a loose smock-type dress. For the latter, you are likely to find a much wider selection of fabrics in the conventional materials.

You can pretty well tell the degree of stretch by pulling the fabric—*in the direction of the stretch*. You should test a piece large enough so that when you pull your hands are at least a foot apart because you can't judge by a small piece of fabric. The cloth should snap back almost immediately.

# New Vistas in Home Sewing

The stretch fabrics have opened up some new vistas for today's generation of women who sew. Before World War II, when silk was widely available, many of us used to make our own main undergarment, the chemise. Today the body shirt, the natural bra and bikini panties have replaced the chemise—and all can be designed and made at home with stretch fabrics.

In the late 1940s, I accidentally came across some rubberized black satin, which at that time was generally not available for home sewing, and made myself a bathing suit. Today you will find in yard goods departments a nylon and spandex stretch tricot that comes in a variety of colors, is a fraction of the weight of that old rubberized satin and, despite its lightness, is opaque. It almost challenges you to make your own bikini or bathing suit. One of the better-known manufacturers of this type of material is Armo Company, an old and established interfacing and lining firm, which has told me it would welcome inquiries from consumers about where the fabric is available retail.

# Sewing with Stretch Fabrics

Sewing with stretch fabrics has some special requirements.

- First, try to choose a pattern with as few seams as possible. Every seam reduces the amount the garment will stretch.
- Don't cut the garment tighter than normal just because it's stretchable. If you stretch a cloth to its limit it will eventually lose some of its recovery.

- Relax the fabric overnight or longer on a flat surface, with no part hanging over the edges.
- Cut with very sharp shears to avoid pulled yarns.
- Make sure the pattern is laid out so that the stretch is in the direction you want it.
- Use at least 14 to 16 stitches per inch and nylon, polyester or silk thread, which have the strength and give needed in the seams.
- If a lining is used, it must also have give—as, for example, tricot has—with the stretch in the same direction as the body fabric.
- Try a lightly looser tension than for regular fabrics, but be sure to test the machine tension on scraps, sewing in the direction of the stretch. Pull the seam; if the thread breaks, adjust the tension.
- Don't use ordinary tape on the hem or seams. It won't give with the fabric.

## Care of Stretch Garments

There are many different factors involved in the care of stretch fabrics: the type of fiber, whether it contains spandex or anidex, the specific stretch process used, etc. No hard and fast rules can be given which will cover all stretch materials. Some may be machine washable, others must be washed by hand or dry cleaned. You must follow the manufacturer's instructions, There is, however, one safe rule for all stretch fabrics: *avoid high heats* in washing, drying or ironing. (Anidex can take somewhat higher temperatures than spandex when, for example, it is blended with cotton, but it is best to play safe.)

For either hand or machine washing, use cool water and a cold-water detergent if the soiling is moderate, a warm-water type if it is fairly heavy.

Never use chlorine bleach on fabrics containing spandex, for they may yellow. Use an oxygen or sodium perborate bleach. Anidex can safely take chlorine bleach.

In machine washing, set the machine for slow agitation—if it has that control—and rinse in cool or lukewarm water with a softener.

The dryer should be at low heat. Remove the garment while slightly damp and finish drying on a hanger. High heat or overdrying may cause serious shrinkage or wrinkles. Spandex combinations are probably safer drip-dried.

If touch-up ironing is needed, use a warm iron and press lightly and rapidly in the direction opposite to the stretch. Don't leave the iron in one position for any length of time.

Generally the stretch fabrics are produced and sold by the firms that make the same fabrics in nonstretch form. Accordingly no special list of wholesale resources is given here.

# ✤XV
# *Durable-Press and Other Special Finishes*

THERE ARE A number of finishes that have limited uses as far as home sewing is concerned but whose properties make them valuable for certain special purposes. First among these are the *durable-press* or *permanent-press* fabrics. The phrases are often used interchangeably because there is—at this writing—no industry standard defining them. In fact, for most consumers they probably should be labeled "permanent press . . . if." Despite the unquestionable attractiveness of clothes that promise to hold a crisp shape, don't lose their pleats even in a downpour and when properly laundered or dry cleaned require no ironing, there are a number of "ifs."

The permanency of the press in most cases will depend on good care labeling instructions and on following them *precisely*. It will depend in part on the responsibility of the fabric's manufacturer or converter. It also will depend on the finishing process used and on the fiber or blend of fibers in the fabric.

There has been much confusion between "wash-and-wear" or "easy care" fabrics and permanent press. The distinction, however, is simple. The so-called wash-and-wear fabrics derive their ease-of-care properties primarily from the fiber (e.g., polyester, nylon or acrylic) or fiber blends and the construction of the fiber, yarn or fabric (e.g., texturizing, double-knit). The permanent-press fabrics, on the other hand, owe their distinctive property to finishing processes that involve both heat and chemicals. And because the shape, creases or pleats are meant to stay in for the life of the garment, they are generally set into the finished suit, dress, blouse, shirt or pants. This means that durable-press clothes—if the press is truly "durable"—cannot be altered without leaving some sign of hem or seam marks. To put it another way: Wash-and-wear clothes remember the original shape of the *fabric* and tend to return to it; durable-press clothes remember the shape of the *finished garment.*

Some durable-press fabrics will be found in yard goods stores but their performance will not be the same as in the best-quality manufactured garments because the woman sewing at home has no way of processing her completed dress, suit or slacks with the high heats required. Nonetheless, fairly satisfactory durable-press performance can be obtained in yard goods designed for sports and casual wear, children's clothes and household articles such as sheets, pillowcases, tablecloths, bedspreads and slipcovers.

# How the Press Is Locked In

For an understanding of how to live without frustration with durable-press clothes some knowledge of the finishing processes and the hows and whys of cleaning are essential.

Three principal methods are used currently in durable- or permanent-press finishing. All depend on the "thermoplasticity" of synthetic fibers, that is, their ability to be set by heat combined with pressure and moisture.

- The first is the *postcure* process. Chemicals are applied to the fabric at the mill. After it has been made into a finished garment and pressed, the clothing manufacturer "cures" the dress, suit slacks or shirt by baking it in a special oven. This sets the pleats or creases and the shape of the garment.

- The second method is known as *precure*. Here the chemicals are applied to the fabric at the mill and partially set by heat, but enough pliability is left in the fabric so that it can be cut, sewn and draped. The finished garment is pressed into its final shape by a special press under very high heat.

- The third process is known as *recure*. Most of the setting is done in the fabric at the mill. After the fabric has been made into a garment, it is partly uncured by steam pressing. The pressed garment is then set into permanent shape by either oven baking or pressing under high heat.

Most of today's durable-press fabrics have a base of polyester blended with either cotton or rayon. The polyester-cotton blend is by far the more popular. Polyester has natural wrinkle resistance, lends itself well to heat setting and adds strength and abrasion resistance to the cloth. Cotton or rayon contribute absorbency and comfort.

## Laundering and Cleaning

Durable-press fabrics demand more attention in laundering and drying than their wash-and-wear counterparts. For example, the thermoplastic properties that permit the fabric to be heat-set into permanent pleats can result, in reverse, in disappearance of the pleats if the dryer is very hot. Also, both polyester and the resins used in curing the fabric tend to cling to grease and oil, so that special treatment is required for that kind of stain. New soil-release finishes applied to durable-press fabrics have helped partially to solve that problem.

With these factors in mind, here are some guidelines for the care of durable-press fabrics that will generally be safe. These are not, however, intended in any way to substitute for the precise care instructions you should get from your retail store.

For best results, durable-press clothes should be laundered in a home washing machine with temperature controls and tumble-dried at warm or medium temperatures. They may also be sent out for dry cleaning, or washed by hand.

If hand-washed, they should never be twisted or wrung while washing or rinsing. Let them soak in detergent and warm water, then rinse thoroughly and squeeze the water out of the garment. Drip-dry on a rustproof hanger or, in the case of pants, by the cuffs on a spring-clip hanger. When dried this way the garment may need a light touch-up with an iron.

Oily or greasy stains should be treated as soon as they happen and, under any circumstances, before the garment is laundered. Sometimes this can be done with a good cleaning fluid, sometimes by pretreating the spot with a liquid detergent and letting it stand overnight. The most cautious authorities recommend sending the garment to be dry cleaned.

Before laundering in a machine, turn the durable-press garment inside out. The reason is that in, say, a polyester-cotton blend, the cotton, which has less strength than the polyester, may wear more with rubbing, leaving the crease or pleated edge a slightly different color than the surrounding fabric.

Always wash whites separately from colored garments. Polyester and chemically cured fibers tend to pick up color in the wash or rinse water.

In machine washing, the water should be from cool to moderately warm. Hot water may be used if the clothes are heavily soiled, but the clothes should be cooled before they are spun, with a final rinse in cool water. If spun while too hot, durable-press clothes may wrinkle. If the garment is to be drip-dried, remove before the spin cycle.

Tumble drying at the proper temperature is a key to retaining the durable press; it fluffs out the wrinkles. The wash-and-wear setting (warm or medium) should be used. If your dryer has only high heat, you will be safer with drip drying. Overloading the dryer will cause wrinkles. Remove clothes as soon as the dryer stops.

## Sewing Durable Press Fabrics

In sewing durable-press fabrics, don't expect to get the same results you see in manufactured clothes where the press is baked in. A few tips:

• Avoid complicated and pleated styles. The pleats won't be sharp and the seams won't lie absolutely flat.

• Use nylon or polyester thread and the finest possible needle adaptable to the weight of the fabric.

• Use 8 to 10 stitches per inch for the heavier fabrics and 10 to 12 for the lighter ones. Durable press generally requires fewer stitches than other fabrics, to minimize puckering.

• Tension on the machine should be as loose as possible to avoid seam puckering.

• Press each seam very carefully with steam as you sew. Wrinkles will be hard to remove.

## Soil-Release Finishes

Soil-release finishes were first introduced in 1966; they were developed originally to solve the soiling problems of durable press which, as noted earlier, tends to absorb oil and grease. They have since been applied to "conventional" synthetic fabrics and blends that resist penetration by water and detergents but soak up oil and grease.

There are a large number of soil-release processes used by the various textile manufacturers. Generally they fall into two categories. In the first, a protective film is formed around the fibers so that oil- or water-borne stains can't get into the fiber itself. In the second, the surface of the fibers is changed chemically so that the fibers "welcome," rather than repel water, allowing the detergents to penetrate and wash away the stain.

In a world of perfect fabrics, a soil-release finish would wash out virtually all spots and stains. And the best of them work well on such annoying stains as grass, lipstick, ink, grease and even red wine. But performances vary and even with a soil-release finish stain removal should not be taken for granted. Spots and stains—especially greasy stains—should be treated promptly, as recommended in the durable-press section of this chapter, and generally all durable-press care instructions should be followed.

Soil-release finishes are different from soil-resistant finishes, which were introduced much earlier. The latter applied to the fabric merely prevent oil- or water-borne stains from soaking into the fiber if they are blotted up quickly.

## Other Finishes

A finish that can be very valuable in home-designed garments is water repellency. Some fabrics—and many manufactured garments—come with this finish already in. But if not, a capable dry cleaning establishment can treat virtually any fabric or garment for you. It won't waterproof the garment, but will improve its ability to shed water without soaking through.

There are a number of new finishes coming on the market which improve the appearance or hand of certain fabrics. One of the latest, introduced in 1972 by DuPont under the certification mark "Nandel," imparts a finish to single-knit Orlon fabrics that makes them look and feel like a fine cotton lisle, with all the softness of that fabric combined with the ease of care of the acrylic fiber. The new finish is also said to help the knit fabric retain its shape better after washing, and to reduce pilling.

Flame-retarding finishes, important in children's sleepwear and such household items as curtains, will be coming on the market, but at this writing it is too early to tell in what quantities fabrics with such finishes will be available retail.

# XVI
## *Special Fibers*

GLASS, METALLIC AND olefin fabrics are not textiles that you will run across every day, but you should know something about them if only to round out your general textile background.

## Glass

The main consumer uses for glass fabrics to date have been in curtains and draperies, where they play a prominent role. They are naturally nonflammable (unless they have been treated with flammable resins), won't shrink, are wrinkle-free, shed dirt easily in washing, dry quickly and never need ironing. They are manufactured in many woven patterns and a large variety of sheers.

Glass is not an apparel fabric. Until very recently all glass fabrics were irritating to the skin and broke easily when creased or bent at a sharp angle. Some new end uses have been opened up, however, by the development of "Beta" yarns which are more flexible and so very fine that they are said to be absolutely nonirritating. Among new consumer uses for these yarns are bedspreads and ironing board covers.

The glass fiber is made from silica sand, limestone, soda ash, borax, boric acid, feldspar and fluorspar. The mixture is melted in a furnace and the molten glass is pulled through a tiny hole at the bottom of the melting kettle and collected on a high-speed revolving device which stretches it into a long, thin filament. Staple-length fibers, for spinning into glass yarn, are created by blowing the filaments with air or steam jets. The staple fibers are five to fifteen inches in length.

Glass is never blended with other fibers, either natural or synthetic. The reason is that processing subjects it to intense heats of more than 1,200° F., and no other fiber can take that. It is this processing that gives the glass fiber its wrinkleproof property.

Dyeing of the glass fabric is usually done with pigment dyes and special bonding resins which are cured in hot ovens to lock them into the fabric. This allows washing, but no articles made of glass fibers should be dry cleaned.

## How to Wash Glass Curtains or Draperies

Wash gently by hand, using a mild soap in warm water. Rinse thoroughly in clean water and squeeze gently before hanging over padded clothes line or shower curtain rod. Rinse the tub in which you washed the curtains or draperies very thoroughly to make sure there are no tiny glass fragments left.

Rehang the curtains while still damp, smoothing out the hems. Do not iron. *Never* dry clean.

## Sewing with Glass Fabrics

Use the loosest tension possible—3 to 5 stitches per inch. The heavier fabrics take the least stitches, the lighter ones more.

Measure accurately and don't cut away the selvedge, because these fabrics won't shrink or stretch.

Use fine-quality mercerized cotton thread and a sharp needle.

Make regular French seams, or use the selvedge for seams.

All heading must be washable, such as a permanent-finish crinoline or Pellon.

Glass fibers were first produced commercially by Owens-Corning Fiberglas Corporation in 1936 (trademark, "Fiberglas"). Glass yarns also are spun by Johns-Manville, Pittsburgh Plate Glass, Ferro Corporation and others.

## Metallic

A glamorous accent in textiles for home and apparel use is the gold or silver glint provided by the metallic fibers. Usually only a very small amount of these fibers is combined in the yarn with other fibers. In terms of care, the main thing to remember is that metallics are highly sensitive to heat and require a cool iron. Washability of the fabric will depend on the other fibers in the cloth. Usually metallic fabrics should be dry cleaned.

Metallic fibers may be made of metal, plastic-coated metal or a core fiber covered by metal. First produced commercially in 1946, metallics are most widely available for fabric use in "Lurex" yarns made by Dow Badische.

# Olefin

Olefin is used mainly in carpets, although it is found occasionally in sportswear and sweaters, slipcovers, blankets, upholstery, knitwear, pile fabrics and hosiery.

There are two types of olefin fiber; one is known as polypropylene, the other as polyethylene. They are derived from propylene and ethylene gases. The polypropylene type is the one most widely used in textile applications.

Properties of olefin include very light weight, abrasion resistance, quick drying (the fibers don't absorb moisture), excellent resistance to stains and to deterioration from chemicals, rot and perspiration. The fibers have a dry hand, and while they won't absorb perspiration, they have a unique ability to draw body moisture away from the skin and up through the fabric to the outer surface. This is a comfort factor. Used as a filling in quilted materials, olefin can provide better thermal insulation than wool. In caring for fabrics that contain olefin you must use caution. You can machine-wash them in lukewarm water, but if they are machine-dried, the lowest possible setting must be used. Gas-fired dryers of the Laundromat type should be avoided. If an article quilted or padded with olefin is dried under high heat, the heat may build up in the filling to a point where a fire could start. Articles made of 100 percent olefin cannot be ironed because of the fiber's extreme sensitivity to heat. If touch-up ironing is needed in articles containing a blend of fibers that includes olefin, use the lowest possible temperature setting.

# ✤XVII
# *Linings and Interfacings*

LININGS MUST CONFORM with the top fabric in cleaning and washing capabilities and must have the proper weight to enhance the style of the garment. For instance, a wool coat will require a firm-bodied lining, while a sheer dress may need the lightest of voiles or organzas.

The fabrics most widely used for linings are rayon, acetate and nylon. White and pastel rayons and acetates in lining weight are sometimes washable, but polyester and nylon clothes require nylon linings for best results, especially in the washing machine.

If the garment will need ironing as well as washing, it is desirable to hem the top and the lining separately for easier pressing. In other words, don't stitch the bottom of the lining to the body of the garment.

Interfacings are used to give body and shape to special areas such as collars, lapels and other parts of the garment that need greater firmness. The interfacings can be either woven or nonwoven fabrics. Woven interfacings must be used where there is stress and pull, such as the reach in the shoulders. Nonwovens are used to stabilize a section of the garment, say, in the neckline or front facings.

Two major firms specialize in making fabrics for interfacings. Pellon Corporation manufactures nonwoven goods—fabrics made of fibers randomly distributed and held together by chemical binders and heat. The fibers used are polyester and nylon and rayon blends. Armo Company makes all types of woven canvasses, using both natural fibers, including goat hair, and synthetics.

The interfacings are available in either straight or biased construction. The biased fabrics are suitable wherever shaping is needed, as in collars and lapels. The straight type is used to keep straight edges from stretching and to firm up sections of the garment that need it.

Interfacing fabrics come in various weights. (Be sure the one you choose is lighter than the covering fabric.) Some are washable, some must be drycleaned. Here again, the selection will depend on the care characteristics of the main fabric in the garment.

Both Pellon and Armo also make "fusible" interfacings. These are pressed onto the body fabric and are used mainly to give stability to small areas, for example, where the buttonholes will go. Pellon does not recommend use of a fusible as substitute for the main interfacings but merely as additional support.

Applying a fusible fabric to the garment requires a specific ironing temperature. You must follow very carefully the application instructions furnished by the manufacturer—these differ from fabric to fabric.

Linings should be so constructed that they do not pull or distort the top of the garment. One way to achieve this in a dress is to join the lining only at the neckline and armholes. In a skirt it should be attached at the waistband.

In coats and jackets, make a pleat in the center back of the lining and attach the lining to the facings without any pull. Everything can be kept in place by making separate hems on the lining and body fabric and tacking them together in a few spots with one-inch crochet threads to allow some play.

Standard linings usually come in plain colors. That should not stop the more venturesome from using colorful prints and novelties for linings, especially if they show. But again, be sure the lining is compatible with the main fabric in terms of care.

## Some Wholesale Resources

Wholesale resources for linings and interfacings include:

*Earlglo, 119 West 40th Street, New York City*: All types of linings, including prints.

*The Armo Company, 206 West 40th Street, New York City*: Very large selection of woven interfacings, fusibles and woven and knitted linings.

*Pellon Corporation, 1120 Avenue of the Americas, New York City*: Leading manufacturer of nonwoven interfacings and fusibles.

# ⚜XVIII
# *Using Colors and Textures for Creative Effects*

IN DESIGNING YOUR clothes, fabric colors and textures can be used to achieve dramatic and highly personalized effects.

## Use of Color

To lay down rigid rules about the use of color in home designing would be to ignore the fact that each of us has different coloring, figure, personality and likes and dislikes. There are, however, some guidelines. The first is that, by fashion tradition, certain colors are best suited for what could be called "styled" garments while others are generally best used in "soft" clothes.

The "styled" colors are black, navy, beige, clear, bright red, gray and brown. The "soft" include the pastels, all shades of yellow and most prints. A few colors can go either way, depending on the garment's design

139

and the current vogue. These include white, purple and various shades of wine and green.

Color can be very effective as an accent to give a dress or other garment special character. But such accents should be used with discretion.

Let's take a simple illustration. Say you have decided to make a dress with a black top and a white skirt. This combination obviously will make the dress stand out more than the same style would in all white or all black. Then you add a yellow belt. This will give the dress sparkle and a professional design touch. But if you are so impressed with the effect of the yellow that you decide to add another touch of it somewhere else in the dress, it will begin to take on an amateurish look. If on top of that you add still another color, you will probably dilute or lose the whole dramatic effect.

For clothes in the styled colors, white is generally the best accent. Depending on the design, you may also be able to use your favorite bright color in one spot—but discreetly.

Pastels combine well with or are accented by white, but a softer effect can be achieved by combining them with other pastels. If you don't trust your sense of color, almost any pastel will combine well with some shade of green. Try putting the different colors together in front of a mirror in the fabric shop. One important thing to remember is that the colors should have the same tone value—i.e., a pale pink will combine well with a light green, but a shocking pink would go better with shocking lime.

When working with pastels, restrictions on the number of colors need not apply. A very popular dress I once designed had a skirt of five colors running in vertical panels from a solid-color bodice. A chiffon evening dress can be given an irridescent look by using layers of several different colors.

Having chosen the colors for the style you have decided on, you can often heighten the effect by using them in an unconventional manner. In a black-and-white dress, for example, the skirt could be made of black-and-white checkerboard fabric or in stripes of black and white, with either a solid black or solid white top.

## Use of Textures

Combining different textures also can produce striking results. Again, picture a black-and-white dress, but with a top of black rib knit and a skirt of white linen—it would have the look of separates. Or consider combinations of opaque and sheer fabrics—say, a velvet top and a chiffon skirt or pique dress with voile sleeves. Then there are the combinations of dull and shiny fabrics, such as crepe and satin. Many other mixtures are possible. Let your imagination and good taste guide you.

There are two cautions, however. First, if the garment is to be washable, the fabrics must be compatible in this regard. Second, make sure the contrasting fabrics can be sewn together without problems. For instance, don't try stitching a heavy skirt to a lightweight bodice that will be pulled out of shape by the weight of the skirt.

## Imaginative Use of Fabrics

Another way of developing original designs is to use fabrics for purposes other than those ordinarily associated with them. For example, you could use denim for a summer evening dress in a long-skirted halter style, perhaps embroidered with white chalk beads. I have also seen cotton lace—usually associated with evening wear—used for beach coats or as patchwork on jackets and skirts, that is, lace interspersed with gingham or other lightweight fabric.

Very often an attractive effect can be achieved by using an unexpected fabric in a conventionally styled garment. An unusual and charming example I once saw was a short pink wool jacket, very simply tailored, lined with narrow bands of lace stitched together. Multi-colored ribbons attached to a band form curtains for windows and doorways in many homes along the Mediterranean and I have seen the idea copied on skirts in New York.

A good source for unusual fabrics is the upholstery department of your favorite store. Here you will find the velours, plushes, carpet-type fancies and other fabrics that can lend an original touch to your clothes. Upholstery fabrics can make very attractive coats, jackets, pants and other types of clothes, depending on the weight of the particular cloth. Some upholstery fabrics come in fairly light weights, such as chintz, an old-fashioned fabric of great charm that lends itself well to dresses and children's wear. The prints on the chintz, fabrics can often be cut out and appliquéd on other fabrics. Chintz, however, does not breathe well and for hot-weather comfort would be better used in the skirt section of a dress, with a more absorbent material for the top.

Quilting and patchwork are other ways of using fabrics imaginatively. The warmth of cotton can be increased by quilting and this is done extensively in a number of countries for economic reasons. In the

United States, quilting is used mainly for fashion effect, to give a thick-and-thin look to the fabric or enhance a design.

## Felt

Felt, a wool fabric produced without weaving or knitting, is also good for special effects. Wool fibers have a tendency to mat solidly and special machines are able to process them into felt. Felt has been used extensively for cut-out appliqués, but it can also make attractive toppers, capes and flared skirts. Felt does not require lining, and since the edges do not ravel, no special finishing is required, although pinking shears can give it an attractive ricrac finish. Various-colored bindings also are popular with felt garments.

## Lace

A fabric that periodically becomes popular is lace. Today lace is made in all fibers and many different widths. While it is still possible to find expensive hand-embroidered laces, most laces are machine-made of cotton, rayon or nylon. The wide laces are used for dresses, or large parts of them, such as skirts, tops or sleeves. The narrow edgings and insertions are used as trim and hem bindings. Some of the narrow laces come elasticized for use where stretch is necessary.

## Make Your Own Fabrics

You can even create your own fabrics. I have already mentioned the idea of sewing narrow strips of lace together to make a lining. A less expensive way of using novelties—such as ribbons, embroidery strips or ric-rac—is to stitch the strips about an inch apart on a backing of *preshrunk* muslin or other inexpensive base fabric. (The preshrinking is essential.) This type of home-manufactured fabric can make a highly original dress or skirt. It can also be used to cover an odd chair or stool and turn it into a conversation piece.

Remember it is the free use of imagination that gives freshness to style and makes familiar things look new. During World War II, when most silk was conscripted by the military, largely for use in parachutes, the brides of airmen occasionally had wedding gowns made of parachute silk—when the groom could obtain it. It was one of the most beautiful cloths ever made and certainly didn't look military on the young brides.

Unfortunately they are not making parachute silk any more, so don't try to find it in a fabric store!

# Index

*Numbers of references to drawings are printed in italic type.*